Las Vegas

The Fabulous
First Century

Lights, camera, action! Las Vegas owes much of its appeal to neon-sign-maker Thomas Young (1895–1971), seen standing (center) in front of the Pioneer Club in the 1940s, one of his many Glitter Gulch creations. (Courtesy YESCO.)

Las Vegas

The Fabulous
First Century

THOMAS "TAJ" AINLAY JR., JUDY DIXON GABALDON

Published by Arcadia Publishing
Charleston SC, Chicago IL, Portsmouth NH, San Francisco CA

Printed in the United States

Library of Congress control number: 2002117433

For all general information contact Arcadia Publishing at:
Telephone 843-853-2070
Fax 843-853-0044
E-Mail sales@arcadiapublishing.com
For customer service and orders:
Toll-Free 1-888-313-2665

Visit us on the Internet at www.arcadiapublishing.com

CONTENTS

FOREWORD

Congratulations to my good friend "Taj" and his co-author Judy, who have written a meticulously researched book about our "can do" successes and our struggles. This book about the history of Las Vegas is not only an accurate account of events in the founding and "creation" of our unique city and county, but a walk down memory lane for those of us who have spent close to 45 years or more living in this extraordinary city and county.

Since my family's move to Las Vegas in 1959, the population has grown almost 3,000 percent. Clark County has grown from roughly 50,000 people in the entire valley to almost 1.6 million people, an astonishing percentage. And while we are all called Las Vegans, the Strip and unincorporated Clark County has become the largest urban county in the United States.

This book is a must-read not just for the pleasure of us old-timers, but more importantly for the many tens of thousands of people who have moved here in the last 10 or 15 years. We have great weather and unmatched opportunities for people who otherwise would not have had them. It is crucial for the maintenance of our outstanding quality of life for them to understand we live in a desert, and that the gaming and rapid growth environment breeds a distinctive culture unlike any other.

- Myrna Williams
Vice-Chair, Clark County Commission

ACKNOWLEDGMENTS

This book would not have been possible without access to the work of the many authors listed in the bibliography. To them we are gratefully indebted for preserving and interpreting the rich history of the Las Vegas Valley for more than 100 years. Similarly, the photographers—who captured and preserved the images of the people and places upon whom our history is based—deserve our heartfelt appreciation.

In the months of preparation that led to the actual writing of the book, we depended heavily upon the resources of the Las Vegas–Clark County Library District. Particularly helpful were the librarians of the Las Vegas Library, who provided access to their Special Collections archives, and of the Sunrise Library, who provided a meeting room for our biweekly research meetings. Special thanks go out to the many institutions that opened their files and records to us, particularly Del Webb Corporation, Young Electric Sign Company, and the Las Vegas Colony of Paiute Native Americans. Visits to the Las Vegas Natural History Museum, Old Las Vegas Mormon Fort State Historical Park, Hoover Dam Visitors Center, Clark County Heritage Museum, and the Nevada State Museum and Historical Society were also most helpful.

Researching and writing a book in the twenty-first century has been made easier by the powers of the Internet. We deeply appreciate those who have made information about Las Vegas and its history available electronically, including: publishers, such as the *Las Vegas Review-Journal*, the *Las Vegas Sun*, and *Las Vegas Life*; organizations, such as Las Vegas Visitors and Convention Authority, University of Nevada (Las Vegas and Reno), and the National Register of Historical Places; and individuals, notably Patrick Weaver, whose Vintage Vegas Postcard Museum is a true treasure chest of historic images, Deanna DeMatteo, and Erik Wunstell. A special note of gratitude goes to the memory of Susan Berman. We also wish to acknowledge the contributions and encouragement of the many people we contacted in the course of preparing the work—not all of whom could possibly be listed here, unfortunately—with special gratitude to David Schwartz, Kathleen War, Peter Michel, Sandra Clerks, Susan E. Searcy, Frank Wright, Kenric Ward, Terrie O'Brien, Steve Mellenthin, and Annette Gaddis.

Lastly, we thank our loved ones, without whose patience and support the work could have neither begun nor been completed. This book is dedicated to our children—Tessera and Shina Ainlay; Jason and Tiffany Burns, and Freddy Gabaldon—to whom we joyfully present the story of *Las Vegas: The Fabulous First Century*.

~ Thomas Ainlay Jr. and Judy Dixon Gabaldon

INTRODUCTION

Las Vegas is unique among cities in America and, at the same time, uniquely American. No other community in the United States—or the world, for that matter—has seen so many dramatic changes in such a short time. From a whistle stop of approximately 1,200 settlers in 1905, to a population expected to number 1.5 million by 2005, its story of growth is one of hardships, challenges and survival, and ultimately huge, undreamed-of successes.

In conducting research for this book, it became apparent to us how many different "histories" of Las Vegas there are—not just the sheer volume of books written on the subject, but the great number of perspectives from which the city's past can be viewed. There is the obvious story of Las Vegas entertainment, the less publicized saga of its military involvement, and the occasionally scandalous records of its civic and business development. There is the little-known Native American history of the region, a downtrodden, then triumphant African-American chronology, an understated Hispanic history, a frequently ignored Asian-American background, and an often-misreported history of Italians, Jews, and Mormons who contributed so greatly to what Las Vegas would become. The history of Las Vegas is political, environmental, architectural, cultural, and even spiritual. At times, it can seem almost mythical, populated by characters so famous (or infamous), they are immediately recognized by a single name—Bugsy, Sinatra, Dino, Sammy, Liberace, and Elvis.

Many of the books we studied included chapters on several of these interpretations, but no single book wove the histories together in a continuous narrative fabric, the way Las Vegas began, grew, and developed into the special place it is today. That became our challenge: to record the past of Las Vegas as a tapestry of perspectives—an encompassing history of community—from prehistory, to the town's unusual founding, to the twenty-first-century metropolis it has become.

Contemporary Las Vegas is astonishing. At night, it is a brilliant cluster of jewels of all shapes, sizes, and colors, glowing in the middle of a vast, black velvet canopy. By day, it is also an amazing sight, almost like a mirage. There is nothing but desert and rugged mountains all around, and then—in the middle of it all—one of the largest and fastest growing cities in the United States . . . truly an enigma.

How could a huge, metropolitan city like this—surrounded by desert terrain inhabited mainly by lizards and cactus—exist? The answers are many, but the main one is simple: water. The area was once a true oasis, with abundant bubbling springs. It drew people here and kept them coming. Water was the reason Las Vegas became a major railroad stop between Los Angeles and Salt Lake City, and why real estate lots were auctioned off to excited bidders a few years into the twentieth century.

Las Vegas has quickly adapted and changed with the times, continually reinventing itself. Sixty years ago, it was "Still a Frontier Town." Today, it has many titles: "Sin City," "Lost Wages," the "City without Clocks," "24/7," and "The Entertainment Capital of the World." But beyond the many names, it is a community of diverse peoples with common goals: to be successful and make this place their home.

Of course, when people think "Las Vegas," they rightfully envision an exciting tourist destination—one of the most popular in the United States. Here, you will find the world's ten largest hotel/casinos. It has been the favorite venue for most popular entertainers of the era, from the early days of Joe E. Lewis, Xavier Cugat, and "Mr. Bojangles" to Wayne Newton and Siegfried and Roy. Showgirl productions still abound, as well as such amazing high-tech, underwater and over-the-top productions as Cirque du Soleil's *Mystere* and "O." Moreover, Las Vegas offers sports (entertainment, participation, and betting) of all kinds, amusement parks, and roller coasters. Las Vegas has also become one of the top centers of epicurean excellence in just a few short years.

Thanks to water and air conditioning (courtesy of Lake Mead and Hoover Dam), Las Vegas now has a hospitable and inviting, exciting atmosphere, which continues to lure millions of tourists and thousands of new residents every month. Some find the allure hard to understand; "It's a fun place to visit, but why would anyone want to *live* here?"

For Las Vegas residents, the attraction is often hard to explain. Something drew them here—an intangible *je ne sais quois* that was and is calling them, like moths to a flame or prospectors to gold. This has been true since the earliest visitors came to the area and settled, despite extreme hardships.

To understand the "allure" of Las Vegas, it would be helpful to stand on a particular plateau at the outskirts of town, on the corner of East Bonanza and Hollywood. One night, just at dusk, when the sun has barely gone down behind the purple mountains to the west and leaves a golden glow in the sky, at that same moment, the lights of the city begin twinkling below.

Behind you is Sunrise Mountain—a symbol of eternity. It was once covered by a vast sea, and then witnessed the period of the dinosaurs. Throughout time, it has not changed. You can see it in the background of old paintings, of the Las Vegas Ranch for example, looking the same—much like a man lying on his back, gazing up at the sky. At the base of this mountain is a modern and glorious, white and gold structure built by the Mormons, the Las Vegas Temple, representing a "higher reward in heaven" perhaps.

Turn around slowly and survey the panorama below. The winding, lighted road called Bonanza, leading down to the cluster of twinkling skyscrapers centered on Fremont Street, looks very much like a yellow brick road leading to an emerald city. "Heaven" is above you; "Oz" is below.

Like Oz, Las Vegas must wear a grand façade—one that continues to draw people like a magnet to discover their own personal dreams. Some find fulfillment, others disappointment. At the end of their journey, they may discover that Oz was not what it seemed. Yet the "façade" that lured them turns out to contain something more valuable than what they had been seeking. They have found themselves in the process of the journey.

This is what Las Vegas represents to those who arrive looking for more than glitter and glamour, or the prospect of instant riches. If they persevere in their search long enough, they find "home." Here they can still make a mark, pursue their Horatio Alger fantasies, and be anything they want to be. Las Vegas may well be the last frontier of the "American Dream"—a place where people can still dream big and dreams really do come true.

Chapter One

VISIONS IN THE DESERT

Las Vegas has always been a magnet for visionaries and dreamers. Even the very first visitors saw it as a shortcut to riches. In 1829, trading company owner José Antonio Armijo persuaded officials in Mexico City to let him embark on a mission that could realize his own dreams of wealth. On November 7, he set out from the Santa Fe area with several dozen Mexican merchants to blaze a new trail to California. He knew manufactured goods could be traded there for livestock at great profit. En route, however, Armijo encountered the same impassable terrain that had stymied eighteenth-century Franciscan explorers before him: deep rivers, steep gorges, and wind-swept expanses of bone-dry desert.

On Christmas Day, a reconnaissance team went out on horseback to seek a way across the Colorado River (Rio Grande) and safe passage through the uncharted Native American territories beyond. They also needed to locate sources of water in the arid regions west. By New Year's Eve, their efforts unsuccessful, all but one of the team members had given up and returned to camp. Armijo dispatched search parties to find their lost scout, but they returned empty handed. The horseman was nowhere to be found.

Then miraculously, on January 7, 1830, a lone rider came galloping up the Yerba del Manso (now the Vegas Wash). The errant scout had returned! During his fortnight away, he had discovered not only the Rio Grande ford the merchants sought, but also a number of water holes that would allow their caravan to cross hundreds of miles of wasteland all the way to the Mojave River. One of those oases was relatively lush with vegetation surrounding a warm, freshwater spring. They would call it "Las Vegas," which in English means "the Meadows." That's how an adventuresome young Hispanic, Rafael Rivera, gambled his life and became the first known "out-of-towner" to see the valley that would one day draw visitors by the millions.

Rivera could not at that time, of course, have imagined the area's future power of attraction. Nor could he have known there had already been many visitors to Las Vegas before him. Ten thousand years ago, in fact, the region was inhabited not only by now-extinct behemoths such as the giant sloth, but also by early man. This knowledge was confirmed in the 1930s when a team of archeologists led by Mark Harrington began excavating Gypsum Cave, so named for the ore extracted from Frenchman's Mountain, roughly 15 miles from the current heart of Las Vegas. Harrington's discovery of crude tools and a fireplace proved human existence here at the time of the Ice Age. Similar discoveries were made at Tule Springs, now known as Floyd Lamb State Park.

In fact, people have lived in Las Vegas Valley since as early as 11,000 B.C., beginning with the Paleo-Indians, who made their homes in shoreline caves and hunted wooly mammoths and bison. This lasted as long as the animals lasted (or became extinct) and until the climate became too arid for habitation. Around 2500 B.C., the climate slowly became habitable again and a newly-evolved Native American society named the Archaic or Desert People began appearing. These people were foragers and they were the behavioral ancestors of the later Paiute people.

Around 300 B.C., a new Native American society, the Basketmakers, or Anasazi, appeared in the Las Vegas area, eventually reaching a height of civilization that was called the "Classic Pueblo" or "Lost City" Period. However, by the year 1000, it had become Nevada's first ghost town for reasons still not clearly understood. During the next 700 years, this area was occupied principally by the Nuwuvi, or so-called Southern Paiute Native Americans. Among this group was a band that called themselves the Tudinu, or Desert People, who made the Las Vegas Valley and its surrounding mountains their home.

Survival in the region was by no means easy for these indigenous people. In the harsh desert and rocky mountain surroundings, they never developed agricultural skills. Nor did they keep grazing animals, which they felt endangered the natural ecosystem and competed for their own food supply. A continuous search for nourishment dominated their lives and kept the Native Americans constantly on the move, which explains why a permanent Tudinu settlement did not exist here when Rivera and later pioneers arrived on the scene.

The Southern Paiute gathered in nomadic bands, recognizing no central tribal leadership. Their homes were temporary structures—frameworks made of poles or boughs covered with branches, reeds, and grass. They foraged for roots, seeds, wild berries, and edible desert grasses. They would hunt bighorn sheep, deer, and rabbit in the Spring Mountains to the northwest of the valley. The forests there also provided them with nourishing plants, medicinal herbs, and a bounty of piñon pine nuts used for roasting and grinding into flour that would sustain them during lean winter months.

Central to Nuwuvi culture is a belief that the Creator bestowed all aspects of nature with life, including rocks, water, and air, as well as plants and animals. They considered the Spring Mountains, their original homeland, to be holy and they would often perform ceremonies in the upper elevations. In particular, the Tudinu band treated the Las Vegas Valley and surrounding environs with the utmost respect.

The Native Americans' free-spirited, independent way of life was shattered by the approach of the White Man to this area. According to tribal history, caravans of traders brought with them horse thieves and kidnappers, highway robbers and slavers, who abducted Paiute children and sold them in New Mexico and California. The Native Americans quickly learned to avoid these interlopers, but they could not avoid their influence. Freshwater springs and streams were polluted. Prime campgrounds were overrun and domestic livestock destroyed local plant life. The outsiders also brought with them new diseases, for which the Paiute had no immunity. The tribe survived, however, and until this day, the Southern Paiute are an integral part of the Las Vegas community.

After 1830, many more explorers and traders headed west through the Nuwuvi lands and their path would become known as the "Old Spanish Trail." Among the earliest of those pioneers was Captain John Charles Fremont, whose name lives on in Las Vegas (Fremont Street), mainly because he kept such interesting and accurate notes of what he found here. Fremont was a bold young officer with the U.S. Army Corps of Topographical Engineers, who were at work on a systematic mapping program of their own. Even though the Las Vegas environs were still part of Mexico, many Americans at that time believed that it was the "Manifest Destiny" of the United States to occupy the entire continent of North America. Empowered by this doctrine of westward expansion, the captain led numerous government-sanctioned expeditions into the Great Basin between 1843 and 1853.

It was May 3, 1844 when Fremont and his party of scientists, scouts, and observers came across the "camping ground of Las Vegas." He described in great detail the two streams of water, 4 to 5 feet deep, which gushed from bubbling springs. He remarked that the water temperature (averaging 72 degrees Fahrenheit) was too warm to be palatable as drinking water, but it made for a delightful bathing experience.

Fremont's meticulous and scientific observations, along with the maps drawn by German cartographer Charles Preuss, resulted in the "Report of the Exploring Expedition to the Rocky Mountains in the year 1842 and to Oregon and North California in the Years 1843–44." This was not only a valuable report, but was also a bestseller in its day and became a vital guide for future explorers and pioneer settlers in the West.

By the middle of the century, someone else had developed a vision for the untamed lands of the Old West: a 46-year-old New England carpenter named Brigham Young. In search of Zion, the final gathering place of his religion's true believers, the so-called "Moses" of the Latter-Day Saints (LDS) had brought his followers by the thousands from the Midwest to Utah in 1847. He claimed as Mormon land the Great Basin, including most of present-day Nevada, and declared it a new state he called "Deseret." Here, the spiritually devout could make their temporal home.

As a key strategy in securing Deseret for his people, Young intended to establish colonies throughout the vast territory. "Men were sent out to locate every spring, stream and lake in that region," wrote Delphine "Mom" Squires in her centennial account of the Mormon expansion. "The famed leader knew that water was the one thing besides brawn needed to make the desert bloom like the rose."

In 1855, Young sent 30 of his missionaries from Salt Lake City to Nevada. They were charged with establishing a fort to protect the Old Spanish Trail—also known now as the Mormon Trail—as it wended its way to the LDS settlement in California's San Bernardino Valley. The trail had been designated by the United States government as a postal route in 1852. According to Thomas H. Thompson and Albert Augustus West, authors of the 1881 History of Nevada:

> The contract for carrying the mail over it was awarded to the Mormons, for whose benefit it had been called into existence. For the purpose of facilitating the carrying upon this route and to gain a supply station near the Potosi lead mine that they proposed to work, a post was established by Brigham Young at the Los [sic] Vegas Spring.

William Bringhurst was the leader of those fort-builders, who brought with them oxen and cows, horses, and plows. They would construct residences, clear fields, and grow crops. They would also teach the local Native Americans the tenets of their faith.

In fact, from the beginning of their arrival in the Las Vegas Valley, the Mormons had a strong connection with the Paiute. According to church doctrine, Native Americans descended from a tribe of Israel, the Lamanites, who migrated to this continent around 600 B.C. Both the Mormons and the Paiute would exert strong influence on the development of modern Las Vegas, but their stay in the valley would not be easy. The two groups would have to lose and regain their homes here before settling in for good.

The missionaries were the first to go. Farming the alkaline land was hard. Separation from families back in Utah caused emotional stress. Conversion of the Paiute became increasingly difficult and raids on the crops became more and more frequent, as the Native Americans sought to drive the white invaders from their lands. Describing the Mormons' hardship in a diary entry, Lorenzo Brown, one of the original settlers, summed up the situation as "rather disheartening." He wrote the following:

> The Committee have selected about 12 acres of land for gardens, giving each person one half acre. The prospect for the land looks slim. Most of the wheat is badly blasted and a great deal of smut potatoes and corn eaten by worms. The land is full of saleratus. To all appearance, there will not be half enough grown to support the mission.

Adding to their difficulties, in February 1856, Bringhurst's fire-and-brimstone leadership was challenged when a group of Mormon miners arrived in the area to tap the ore of Mt. Potosi that could be smelted into bullets. Led by a strong-willed lead digger named Nathaniel Jones, they needed to be fed, but contributed little to the settlement's economy. According to John Steele, designer of the original Mormon Fort, "There was a storm between [Bringhurst and Jones] calling each other anything but gentlemen."

In March 1857, many of the Las Vegas defenders returned to Salt Lake City, where U.S. Army troops had invaded Brigham Young's unrecognized dominion under orders from President James Buchanan. Eighteen months later, the missionaries who remained evacuated Las Vegas after a band of Native Americans stole their harvest, leaving them to face winter starvation. The Fort was abandoned, but its important role in local history would soon resume as a much larger historical event played out: the Civil War.

Nevada was officially considered a territory when the country's "slave states" seceded from the Union in 1861. Fewer than 100 African Americans (only 44 by the 1860 census) lived in the region then, most of them in Virginia City and Carson City, where they had formed their own social clubs and churches. The issue of slavery would probably never have affected Las Vegas at all, but for the vision of a very determined man in Washington, D.C.: President Abraham Lincoln.

With the war between North and South escalating and its outcome unclear, Lincoln found himself one vote shy of the 27 needed to ratify his anti-slavery amendment. If Nevada entered the Union as a "free" state, it could provide that swing vote. There was only one problem: with the nation's lowest concentration of urban residents and most-scattered rural population, the territory counted only 16,857 citizens, including an estimated 10,000 Native Americans, who were not actually interviewed in the 1860 census. Nevada did not meet the minimum size requirement for statehood, not even after annexation of acreage from Utah in 1862.

Be that as it may, and despite opposition from many local voters who preferred the far-from-Washington freedom that territorial status conferred, political wheeling and dealing eventually got Lincoln the concessions he wanted. On October 31, 1864, the President proclaimed Nevada the country's 36th state. On February 16, 1865, just two months before Lincoln's assassination, the 13th amendment to the Constitution abolishing slavery was ratified by the new state. It became law in December that year.

Oddly enough, Las Vegas itself was not part of the original "battle born" State of Nevada. When Arizona was formed as a separate territory out of land drawn from New Mexico in 1863, the sun-drenched valley fell within its new borders. Not until 1867 did the federal government finally cede from Arizona 12,225 square miles to form a triangular tip for Nevada, extending south to the Colorado River and including Las Vegas.

By then, the Old Mormon Fort, abandoned in 1858, had seen quite a few changes. In anticipation of Confederate recruitment activities in the Southwest, the United States government confiscated the post in late 1861 and designated it "Fort Baker," honoring an early casualty of the Civil War, Colonel Edward Dickinson Baker of Pennsylvania. Functioning mainly as a temporary camp, Fort Baker served to deceive spies and enemy sympathizers in California, who were led to believe it garrisoned four full companies—three cavalry and one infantry. Colonel James Henry Carleton, who had previously led ruthless campaigns against the Paiute, supposedly commanded the First California Infantry there and he took great pains to announce skirmish drills and target practice, making the outpost seem much more active than it really was. The commander even had goods on supply trains marked "Fort Baker," although their actual destination was Fort Yuma. The tiny patrols that bivouacked at the sham arsenal were made out to be a virtual army.

By 1865, the fort's purpose had been served and it was acquired by a former miner named Octavius Decatur Gass. His luck as a Forty-Niner in California's El Dorado gold rush had not panned out, but in the years immediately following the Civil War, Gass prospered by tearing down most of the old Mormon structures, planting an orchard, raising a herd of cattle, irrigating the land, and farming. Paiute workers harvested his grain, vegetables, and fruit. Passing wagon trains purchased supplies from the enterprising rancher, including his delicious homemade wine.

Gass used his profits to buy more Las Vegas–area land and became involved in local politics, gaining election to the Arizona legislature for four terms in 1865 through 1868. The fact that Las Vegas and his home were now part of Nevada's newly-formed Lincoln County did not faze him in the least. Initially, he refused to pay Nevada taxes and he continued to report to the Arizona government as the representative of its unofficially anointed Pah-Ute County until 1870.

The shift in the legislator's allegiance to Nevada came about in 1871, when Gass fell in love with Mary Virginia Simpson, originally of Missouri. She, too, had settled on former Mormon property along the Old Spanish Trail in Moapa, 50 miles across the barren wastes northeast of Las Vegas. They courted. They married. They settled at the Las Vegas Ranch and had six children there over the course of nine years.

But eventually, the miner's bad luck returned. Nevada demanded back taxes from the former Arizonan. The Gass's spacious house, Chinese and Bavarian cooks, and Paiute house servants came at a cost. There were rumors of extravagance, poor management, and excessive generosity to visitors. Under heavy debt and unable to keep up mortgage payments in August 1879, Gass scrambled for a way to save his home. He turned for help to the town of Pioche, where a successful rancher-cum-businessman was willing to extend a loan of $5,000 in gold against the ranch's unencumbered deed as collateral. That loan kept the Gass family going for another year and then for nine months more on an extension. But when the cash-strapped homesteader failed to repay the loan plus interest on May 2, 1881, the deed to the old fort-turned-ranch defaulted to lender Archibald Stewart. It is a tale of dreams, romance, and reversal of fortune that would become commonplace in Las Vegas history. In fact, Stewart himself would provide its next page.

The 640-acre Las Vegas Ranch was more than just a home for people, animals, and crops. It also included a store that served the basic needs of travelers stopping along the Mormon Trail, the forerunner of "tourist hospitality services" to come. Although he was the ranch's new owner, Stewart did not want to live there. Happy at home in Pioche with his wife Helen and their three children, he entrusted the management of the new property to two partners, an arrangement which turned out to be short-lived. Before a year had passed, the partners had a disagreement and split up. In the spring of 1882, Stewart moved his family to the ranch. Two years later, he would be the focus of the first Las Vegas murder mystery.

Apparently, one July afternoon in 1884, Stewart had traveled 2 miles from his home to visit the ranch of a neighbor, Conrad Kiel. There, he encountered one of his own former ranch hands, Schuyler Henry, who shot and killed Stewart. Henry insisted it was self-defense, that his overbearing ex-boss had come there with a rifle, intending to punish him for quitting and joining up with Kiel, who allegedly was away when the shooting took place. A jury believed Henry and dismissed the charges in August. However, Helen Stewart insisted for the rest of her life that it was cold-blooded murder, a conspiracy between Henry, Kiel, and a gunslinger named Hank Parrish, who had been at the ranch when the body was found. Although he was a potential eyewitness, Parrish conveniently disappeared from the area by the time of the trial. The case was closed with dozens of questions unanswered.

The intrigue did not end, however, with Archibald Stewart's death. Another murder occurred on the Kiel Ranch 16 years later. This time, the dead were the two sons of Conrad Kiel, Edwin and William. Supposedly, animosities between the Stewarts and the Kiels had long-since been (at least outwardly) resolved and, on October 11, 1900, Helen Stewart and accompanying ranch hands had traveled to the Kiel Ranch to "pay a visit and replenish their supply of tobacco."

Reportedly, they found the two Kiel Brothers, both dead, with a pistol next to the hand of one of them. For quite some time, it was assumed that one of the brothers shot the other and then, in remorse, shot himself; therefore, it was widely considered to be a murder-suicide.

However, in the mid-1970s, the brothers' bodies were exhumed by researchers at the University of Nevada, Las Vegas (UNLV) and forensic analysts declared that they both had been murdered—both shot in the back of the head. So, it was a double murder. But who was or were the murderer(s)? Perhaps someone in the Stewart family, seeking revenge? Another mystery shall remain unsolved.

Murder or not, ownership of the Las Vegas ranch passed on to Archibald Stewart's widow after her husband's death in 1884. This cruel twist of fate had for the first time placed a woman center stage in Las Vegas history and she turned out to be every bit the match for her new role.

Helen Stewart, by all accounts, was an amazing woman. She was described as being delicate and fragile in appearance, "like a Dresden doll," yet her inner strength and fortitude belied that outward façade. Over the next 20 years following her husband's death, she managed the ranch and—being pregnant when her husband Archibald was murdered—gave birth to her fifth child. It was said that the widow Stewart often tried to sell her inherited property to move her family back to "civilization," her home in Galt in the Sacramento Valley of California, but to no avail; she eventually accepted her role with grace in the often uninhabitable conditions.

Stewart was known far and wide as a magnanimous hostess at her ranch, providing food and a place to rest for weary travelers. She made a home for her family and enlisted a teacher to tutor her children. She became an avid Native American basket collector and friend to the Paiute, who would cut hay, haul wood, and work as her cowboys. In 1885, no fewer than 23 Paiute lived on the Las Vegas Ranch and, though they adopted some aspects of the ranch's "foreign culture," they did not abandon their ways and continued to hunt and gather plants right up to the turn of the century.

At age 14, Stewart's son Archibald, named after his father, was killed when thrown from a horse. It was said that Helen never got over his death. Still, she survived admirably and reminded her children that one day things would change. The obituary, following Helen Stewart's death on March 6, 1926, included this revealing paragraph:

> Mrs. Stewart was a woman of vision and often told her children just to be patient, that civilization would find them, that she could see the glint of the rails, the smoke of the trains, and homes and church spires in the grain field on the hill. Her vision became a reality when a large part of the old ranch, with its adobe buildings, together with the big spring were sold to the Los Angeles & Salt Lake Railroad Company, and the town of Las Vegas was born May 15, 1905.

Chapter Two

DESTINY'S WATER STOP

At the turn of the twentieth century, the official population of the Las Vegas Valley, which did not count Native Americans at that time, was a mere 30 persons. There were no rich mines to draw prospectors. Raising cattle and farming in the arid, alkaline land had attracted few settlers. But there were already rumors in the desert wind of a project that would bring immigrants to the region by the hundreds, turning the scattered ranches into a true community. The railroad was coming!

Rumors of plans to connect Los Angeles and Salt Lake City by rail had been circulating since 1881. The railroad would follow the general path of the Old Spanish Trail, later called the Mormon Trail. The Union Pacific saw great value in expanding its transcontinental network to the southern corner of the west coast, but economic slumps in the 1880s, followed by depression and financial panic in 1893, then the Spanish-American War in 1898, caused the work to stop each time it seemed to be getting started. Bankruptcy and subsequent reorganization of the rail company kept the Union Pacific from securing the proposed route before a competitor came on the scene—an ambitious, copper-rich senator from Montana named William Andrews Clark.

In 1901, the wealthy politician cobbled together a new entity, the San Pedro, Los Angeles, & Salt Lake Railroad (SPLA&SL), buying out a number of small local railroads that made up the Los Angeles Terminal Line and—by making good on the Union Pacific's unpaid land taxes—acquiring grades previously abandoned in Lincoln County, Nevada. Legal disputes between the two mighty rail companies followed, each claiming the right to lay track through Nevada. Eventually, Clark's SPLA&SL prevailed, but not before the bitter negotiations escalated to violence between rail workers. Stoppages lasted for months on end. A final settlement was not reached until July 1903 and construction fell far behind schedule.

Even after tempers had cooled, working on the railroad was still difficult. The laborers lived in movable camps and were paid $2 per 10-hour day if they were white, 25¢ less if they were Mexican or Native American. Describing the lives of the track-builders, Rebecca Palmer, an archaeologist with the Nevada State Historic Preservation Office, wrote the following:

> Outside the modest tent shelters, laborers constructed small warming
> fires in the many washes that surrounded most of the camps. At least six

commissary cooks employed by the contractors completed food preparation. Canned fruits and vegetables, syrup, bacon, locally grown potatoes and onions were the typical fare. Recent archaeological excavations revealed that they butchered and prepared sheep, goats, wild game, and locally grown cattle from the Las Vegas Ranch to supplement the usual tinned fare. They also baked bread in dome-shaped ovens constructed from locally available rock. Archaeological excavations have revealed creative reuses of available materials, suggesting that supplies were quite limited. Archaeologists have found 25-pound blasting powder tins shaped into baking pans, used as insulation for outdoor hearths, punctured and refashioned in sieves or sifters, and bundled together for sleeping platforms.

Water for consumption and other purposes came from water wagons, concrete-lined cisterns, and after 1905, from a pipeline constructed by the railroad. Despite the rules and best intentions of the construction company and their contractors to enforce prohibition, residents of the camps did consume alcoholic beverages. Entrepreneurs quickly established temporary saloons next to the camps or in nearby locations.

En route to eventual victory, Clark took a page from Brigham Young's Deseret strategy and sought to control water rights along the rail route. The springs of Las Vegas were an obvious target. A stop there would be almost exactly halfway between the Salt Lake and Los Angeles terminals. Helen J. Stewart, owner of the Las Vegas Ranch, had previously accepted an offer to purchase her property from the Oregon Short Line Railroad, a subsidiary of the Union Pacific, which also obtained rights to the Kiel Ranch. However, that deal fell through during the railway's bankruptcy period.

In 1902, Clark paid Stewart $55,000 for the rights to all 1,840 acres of her ranch, except "Four Acres" (the Stewarts' private burial ground) and a separate lot of 160 acres. That purchase included the water rights to Big Springs—the source of Las Vegas Creek and the most important water hole in the valley. In the course of negotiations, SPLA&SL's representative William McDermott hired local civil engineer John T. McWilliams to survey the Stewart estate.

McWilliams had come to the region from Canada in 1894 to work on projects in Goodsprings, Nevada. He found undeeded forest land in the Spring Mountains area and shrewdly laid claim to 1,300 acres of it for himself. (The Southern Paiute tribe's ownership of their ancestral home was not recognized in those days.) Timber rights had been McWilliams's main interest in the land. But as he surveyed the Las Vegas Ranch for the railroad, a new desire for property overtook him. A townsite was needed. If he could somehow obtain a nearby parcel, who better than a local surveyor to lay out the grounds for homes and businesses? The biggest problem would be access to water, but the engineer knew an artesian water belt ran under the valley floor. Wells could provide what the railroad would not relinquish.

In 1904, McWilliams convinced Helen Stewart to sell him 80 of her remaining acres, close to the Las Vegas Creek and convenient to the roads leading to the mining towns of Goldfield, Rhyolite, and Tonopah. By October, when the SPLA&SL tracks from Caliente, Nevada had reached south to the Las Vegas Ranch, McWilliams began advertising lots for sale in what today is the area bounded by A and H Streets, Bonanza and Washington—the west side of the tracks. Throughout the winter months, sales were brisk and, by early 1905, the local population surpassed 1,500. Many of the buyers were teamsters, who worked the old mining trails. Some were rail workers. Others were simply attracted by McWilliams's offer of cheap land with little down payment. Immigrants seeking to get in on the railroad boom included Chinese and Mexicans, Native Americans, Greeks, Irish, Austrians, Finns, Italians, and Spaniards. They lived in tents, for the most part, and the McWilliams Townsite soon earned the label "Ragtown."

Meanwhile, on the other side of the tracks, Senator Clark and his newly formed Las Vegas Land and Water Company (LVL&WC) had no intention of letting a local opportunist determine the location of "their" town. Work on the Caliente–Las Vegas section had required the hiring of 500 men and the subcontracting of 1,200 others. They had invested heavily in getting the tracks to and through the Las Vegas Valley, and they would be the ones to reap the benefits.

Never a true resident of Las Vegas, Clark had several men looking out for his interests in the valley. One was his brother J. Ross Clark, who managed the railroad as its vice president and lived with his family in Las Vegas as president of LVL&WC until 1925. Another representative was Walter Bracken, who seemed to run everything, but who closely followed orders from the company.

Bracken took up residence at the Las Vegas Ranch in 1904. In addition to his duties as the railroad, water, and land agent, he also served as postmaster of the first Las Vegas Post Office, which had previously been known as Bringhurst Post Office in the 1850s and renamed the Los Vegas Post Office (to distinguish it from the one in the Las Vegas, New Mexico) from June 24, 1893 until December 9, 1903. The last spikes linking the east and west sections of the SPLA&SL railroad were driven unceremoniously in Jean, Nevada, 23 miles southwest of Las Vegas, on January 30, 1905, then a symbolic gold spike was put in place by Chief Engineer Edward G. Tilton. Six days later, the first through train departed Salt Lake and made the two-day run to Los Angeles. A special load of excursion passengers made the return trip on April 15 and, on May Day, the route was formally opened for regular service.

Passenger trains would continue operations through Las Vegas uninterrupted for the next 66 years. The railroad depot's The Beanery restaurant would serve as a social gathering and meeting place for the townsfolk and it would be the site of the valley's first long-distance telephone call received in 1929.

Even as the railroad was nearing completion, Bracken was drawing up plans under orders from the Montana senator for the Clark Las Vegas Townsite. It would feature 38 blocks measuring 300 by 400 feet, with 80-foot-wide streets in between and 20-foot-wide alleyways within. Two of the segments, Blocks 16 and 17, were zoned for the sale and consumption of alcohol. Block 20 was reserved for future public facilities—a library and a courthouse. The townsite comprised the area bounded by what are now Fifth and Main Streets and Stewart and Garces Avenues. Apart from the promise of a plentiful water supply, it had the advantage of close proximity to the rail yards and planned depot. What's more, free lots would be given to religious organizations of any denomination willing to establish churches there.

On May 8, 1905, the first lots in the Clark Las Vegas Townsite were put on sale. The response was so overwhelming—more than 3,000 offers at between $100 and $300 an acre—that Bracken and his bosses decided to hold a land auction, rather than sell the property directly. In newspaper advertisements, the LVL&WC announced special rail excursion fares to bring bidders to the event—$16 round-trip from Los Angeles, $20 from Salt Lake, which would be rebated to the actual buyers. A crowd of over 3,000 showed up, cash in hand, on the morning of May 15, 1905, and the frenzied bidding commenced under the gavel of professional auctioneer Ben E. Rhoades.

It started out as a mild enough day, but by 3 p.m., the temperatures had soared to 110 degrees, bringing the event to an earlier-than-planned conclusion. When Rhoades brought down the final gavel of the day, the town of Las Vegas officially came into existence. By then, from a pool of 1,200 lots, a total of 176 had been sold. Winning bids ranged as high as $1,750 for prime real estate on the northeast corner of Main and Fremont, and the day's revenues totaled $79,566. On the next day, most of the remaining land sites were sold off at specified prices, bringing the total sales to $265,000. Lots that found no buyers were put on offer in Los Angeles and Salt Lake through agents for the land company. Las Vegas was finally off and running.

Once the people in the McWilliams Townsite became aware of the more advantageous location to the east, many grabbed their tents and belongings and moved over to the more prime pieces of property. The entire Imperial Hotel building was torn down and reassembled in the new townsite. Within three days of the auction, local newspaper The Las Vegas Age defected, moving its fireproof building on rollers to Clark's side of the tracks. The "original" townsite suffered a great deal from the exodus. Those who couldn't afford the move stayed behind and certain businesses—mostly cafes, stores, hotels, and stables—kept going. The feud between McWilliams and the railroad was on.

Although Clark and his organization were the obvious winners in the initial confrontation, their victory came at a price. More than a few of the bidders were land speculators from California, out to make a quick profit. After experiencing the desert heat, they packed up their bags and went home, never to return. Many of the local winners felt they had paid unfairly high amounts due to the Californians' price-hiking bids. Lots valued at a few hundred dollars had been sold for up to $1,200, leaving the new owners with less cash for construction and fewer neighbors to do business with. As a result, the commercial development of the blocks east of Fremont Street lagged far behind expectations. That area would not flourish for a quarter century. Only a few commercial blocks near the tracks, residential sections off Fremont between Fourth and Fifth, and the soon-to-be notorious Block 16, thrived in the weeks following the auction. In those areas, a crusade of wild construction ensued as houses, saloons, hotels, a new post office, and the town's first bank sprang up out of nowhere. Many of the wood-frame structures were considered "permanent," but canvas tents—easily relocated from the Westside—were still prevalent in the new town, as was the stench of horses and burros and the presence of flies. Some of the new businesses would not last even a month.

On June 6, a fire threatened the town's start. It seems that a kitchen helper at Chop House Bill's tried to refuel a lighted stove, resulting in a blaze that destroyed four buildings before a bucket brigade could put it out. Less than two weeks later, sparks from a locomotive led to a potentially disastrous fire in the rail yard's coal chutes. Insurance companies of the day would not assume the risk of issuing fire policies in the dry, desert community, which had no formal fire brigade, so any losses were total. And fire was not the only danger. Summer storms and floods damaged the railroad in July and August, causing closures that hurt the water stop's economy. In time, the level of the tracks would need to be raised to avoid damage from such natural disasters.

Taking little solace in the railroad's woes, McWilliams had problems of his own. On September 5, 1905, his townsite experienced a huge fire—origins unknown, foul play suspected—that all but destroyed the developer's dream. The Westside did not quite disappear with the flames, but it never recovered completely. Rather than give up hope, McWilliams continued to battle for water rights for his 80 acres and eventually won. In 1906, when Washington politicians, perhaps goaded by Senator Clark, attempted to rescind the surveyor's Spring Mountain land deed, McWilliams wrote a letter directly to President Theodore Roosevelt and had the judgment overturned. He would later win another minor battle with the railroad when he discovered a portion of their new ice house overlapped his own townsite property. Rather than pay McWilliams $1,000 for the land, Walter Bracken ordered his men to cease construction and move the facility to another location. The feuding would continue till McWilliams's death in 1951.

Where McWilliams failed as an urban developer, he excelled as a conservationist. He successfully stopped the rail company from polluting Las Vegas Creek with cesspool water in 1912. His instincts enabled him to develop Lee Canyon on Mt. Charleston later, in the 1930s, from land he had originally surveyed and laid claim to in 1902, protecting it from loggers and opening trails to hikers, campers, and nature lovers. It is now the Toiyabe National Forest. Over time, he drew up more than 3,000 maps of the area and remained a staunch advocate of Las Vegas and its environs. Though never a recognized town leader, he was always a force to be reckoned with. In 1927, McWilliams summed up his feelings for the fledgling community, saying, "I gladly give my time for the future of what will be a magic city."

It was William A. Clark, on the other hand, whose name was given to the new governing district in 1909, when Lincoln County was divided in two. The three-man commission that headed the county seat in Pioche had been finding it increasingly difficult to oversee the growth under their jurisdiction, which included two towns with populations over 1,000 (Caliente in the north and Searchlight in the south), as well as Las Vegas. Road maintenance, fire departments, peace-keeping, liquor licenses, sewage disposal, and all the minutiae of governing a growing new town could not be properly handled from 190 miles away. Las Vegans wanted the county divided and their town designated the government center for the southern half.

Instrumental in the fight to form Clark County was Edward W. Clark (no relation to the Montana family), a freight-forwarder who had set up his business headquarters in Las Vegas when the town was first formed. Clark was an admitted "behind the scenes" kind of leader, but he would rise to prominence by running the town's first telephone and power companies, and later its main bank. He was elected Lincoln County treasurer in 1906, inheriting responsibility for over $600,000 in debt, which had been incurred as mining operations in Southern Nevada diminished, tax revenues fell, and bonds for a costly courthouse matured.

When Pioche established its own bank in 1908, the commissioners demanded that county funds be transferred there from the First State Bank of Las Vegas (FSBLV), where they had been diverted from a Salt Lake bank on the treasurer's order. Clark refused to move the money from FSBLV. That and his affiliation with a group of local separatists called the Lincoln County Division Club cost him reelection later in the year. But that did not stop Clark from politicking. Many Nevada state legislators were favorable to the idea of dividing Lincoln County. Lobbying by Division Club members, along with a case of Yellowstone Whiskey (allegedly paid for by Clark), may have helped them drum up the support needed for a "yes" vote. In February 1909, the lawmakers approved the division, giving birth to Clark County on July 1.

The town of Las Vegas went wild in celebration. Bell-ringing, fireworks, band music, speeches, races, hose fights, an open-air concert, and a formal ball at the recently opened Opera House on the second floor of the Thomas Department Store marked the occasion. It was said to be the biggest festival ever held in Nevada. Despite opposition from the mining community of Searchlight, 55 miles south, the Silver State's "one-day wonder" had gone from a dusty collection of vacant lots to the

Clark County seat in less than 50 months. The SPLA&SL had recently announced it would be hiring 500 additional workers and spending $400,000 to create machine and maintenance shops on the west edge of town. Construction on 65 new cement-block cottages for the workers had begun, with plans for as many as 120. The town's population was expected to grow by 1,200 to 1,500, and a Las Vegas Promotion Society was formed to extol the many benefits of locating businesses there. It is little wonder that residents soon began referring to Las Vegas as "The City of Destiny."

Of the many people present at the 1905 auction, several would have a lasting influence on that destiny. Among them was Chicago native, second-generation Swiss-American Peter Buol, who would inevitably be remembered as Las Vegas' "one-man chamber of commerce." Buol came to the valley by stagecoach a few years before the railroad was completed. He had already gained and lost a small fortune—$100,000 he won in an 1892 lottery at age 19 was quickly spent—leading him to several years working in food service before moving west in 1901. He saw opportunity in mining, insurance, and real estate operations in southern Nevada, but like William Clark, John McWilliams, and Brigham Young before him, he knew water was the key to fortune here. If the railroad refused to extend the supply of water beyond the lands it controlled, there was money to be made in getting it to those outside the townsite. In November 1905, Buol established the Vegas Artesian Water Syndicate. By drilling wells into the aquifer beneath the desert floor, he could provide what the railroad denied.

By 1910, Buol was able to purchase land at Sixth and Fremont, just beyond the LVL&WC's precincts, where his syndicate brought in a large artesian well. That meant the property between what is now Las Vegas Boulevard and Ninth Street could be developed as home sites. Within months, the area became highly desirable as a residential neighborhood and Buol was again on his way to becoming a wealthy man. By then, however, Las Vegas was feeling far less fortunate.

Despite the euphoria of the summer of 1909, all did not go smoothly for the new county seat. As the price of independence, Clark County was saddled with $430,000 of the old Lincoln County debt. That might have been manageable in a thriving economy, but the very survival of Las Vegas was soon threatened by unforeseen circumstances. Snows melting in the Nevada mountains during late December caused a catastrophe on January 1, 1910, as a huge flood swept across nearly 100 miles of tracks in Lincoln County. Bridges, rail ties, rolling stock, and buildings were all washed away. The route between Las Vegas and Salt Lake was virtually destroyed. The damage was so extensive, in fact, it would take until June to repair it.

As the early months of 1910 dragged on, the railroad maintenance crews in Las Vegas were laid off. Payrolls dried up. Businesses closed. By the time the decade's national census was taken, the town whose population had been exploding a year earlier saw its number of residents fall to just 945. Construction on an eagerly anticipated new grammar school was delayed. When a fire destroyed the existing school, teachers and students had no choice but to hold classes in the Methodist church. Then, across from the rail depot another fire broke out, burning the Overland Hotel to the ground.

As much as it needed water and the railroad, Las Vegas also needed something else to survive. Peter Buol summed it up: "Ability doesn't count, knowledge is useless, experience has no worth without the driving force of optimism." Boundless optimism is exactly what Buol brought to his own life and work. Perhaps he could infuse his neighbors with it.

By January 1911, rail services had been completely restored on the SPLA&SL and the Las Vegas railroad shops went into operation. To hasten its return of prosperity, the town petitioned for recognition as a city under state law and was granted that status on March 11. According to the bill signed by Governor Tasker Oddie, the newly incorporated city would be governed by a mayor and a board of four commissioners, modeled after the government of Galveston, Texas. A special election was held in Las Vegas on June 1 to approve the new charter and choose the city's first mayor. By a margin of 35 votes, that mayor would-be well-digger Peter Buol.

One of Buol's first acts was to issue sewer bonds and raise $40,000 for badly needed sanitation services. Construction soon resumed on the long-awaited elementary school and, by the fall of 1911, the Fifth Street Schoolhouse, completed at a cost of $30,000, would be hailed as the "best schoolhouse in the State." Organizing a well-equipped fire brigade was also high on the mayor's agenda and, although his salary for governing the city was only $15 a month, Peter Buol played a very visible role in all community affairs. With gusto and infectious enthusiasm, he created a role model for all who would follow in his footsteps.

Equally important throughout Buol's tenure until May 1913, his syndicate continued to water the soils surrounding Las Vegas, bringing a secondary industry to the valley—farming. Given proper irrigation, fruit, grain, and vegetables could be grown here. Alfalfa, with up to six harvests a year, quickly became a profitable local crop. Word of the new farming opportunities spread so far and wide, it soon attracted the first colony of Japanese immigrants to Las Vegas. The City of Destiny was back on track.

Quite cognizant of that destiny was Minnesotan Charles Pember Squires. He had arrived in the valley from Redlands, California, in 1905, with $25,000 in borrowed money on one of the very first trains passing through, intent on establishing a number of early commercial interests in the area. He stayed the night at Ladd's, one of the very first tent hotels opened on February 13, 1905 and operated by Captain James H. Ladd. It featured four double beds, offering an eight-hour stay for two people (usually strangers) for $1 apiece. Besides making payment, the hotel also required that the potential hotel client be "not scratching." Bugs and lice were most undesirable and any visitor caught itching in front of the hotel stove was immediately sent packing.

Destiny's Water Stop

Quite likely inspired by Ladd's ability to earn something for nothing, Squires decided to begin his Las Vegas ventures by acquiring a prime piece of land and creating a hotel of his own. He successfully obtained a lot at the 1905 auction on North Main Street near Stewart Avenue and promptly erected a massive tent he named the Hotel Las Vegas. Much larger and more substantial than its surrounding neighbors, the canvas-covered structure was first-class by desert standards, with wood-plank floors and a front porch. It also had a dining room, a kitchen, 30 guest rooms, and a dormitory.

Squires and his investment partners were similarly responsible for the creation of the town's First State Bank, which they hired Los Angeles banker John S. Park to run. Squires built a home for himself and his wife and family on the corner of Fourth and Fremont. Then he did something that surprised even himself: he bought the town's weekly newspaper, *The Las Vegas Age*, from owner C.W. Nicklin for $2,300 and became the town's crusader. "Perhaps," he reckoned, "I could help revive the poor, sick little town."

Squires' move to the editorship of the *Age* placed him squarely in the center of Las Vegas affairs. In 1907, he served on the finance committee of the Division Club. In 1910, he helped draft the city charter for presentation to the state legislature. His opinions were eagerly sought by politicians and business tycoons alike. But it was as a newspaperman that he "sold" Las Vegas to newcomers and investors and earned his reputation as the "Father of Las Vegas." C.P. "Pop" Squires, along with his wife Delphine, affectionately known as "Mom," became the most revered of the community's celebrities. Squires literally had his finger on the pulse of everything new and important to the city. He was involved in Las Vegas becoming the Clark County seat; he was instrumental in the new Consolidated Light and Power Company that "electrified" Las Vegas; and just when the city was beginning to follow the fate of many other boomtowns, by disappearing again into the desert from whence it came, he became central to the plans for building a dam on the Colorado River—a project that would propel Las Vegas through the Great Depression and into its destined future.

Among the four city commissioners who listened to Squires's advice and worked closely with Mayor Buol from 1911 to 1913 was the son of another Swiss immigrant, also born in Illinois in 1873, Ed Von Tobel. Like the mayor and the editor, he had been present at the 1905 auction and, along with St. Louis friend Jake Beckley, he had managed to secure a lot in the townsite for just $3 cash! In the scorching heat of that May afternoon, auctioneer Rhoades had spiced up the bidding by offering to credit the value of the winner's train ticket against a 25 percent down payment. With a successful bid of $100 for his lot, Von Tobel happily surrendered his $22 ticket stub and three singles for a piece of destiny.

Where Buol's Las Vegas future was to be found in water, Von Tobel's was to be in wood. The growing town needed lumberyards and that was his specialty. Unfortunately, seven other lumber companies moved into the townsite at the same time as Von Tobel and Beckley. Competition for contracts was fierce, but demand was steady over the next four years as materials were needed to build all the accouterments of a modern twentieth-century town, including two schools, two churches, six hotels, a new rail depot, a theatre, fifteen stores, a brace of meat markets, half a dozen restaurants, a bakery, a plumbing shop, a blacksmith's, offices for five attorneys, two doctors and two dentists, three barber shops, a couple of billiard halls, two newspapers, and eleven bars and saloons. Some structures, such as the original county government building erected in 1909, were made of concrete block, and the most fashionable houses in town incorporated brickwork, but wood was by far the building material of choice.

Jake Beckley's brother Will also arrived in Las Vegas in 1908 and opened a small clothing store in a tent house that doubled as his home. Two years later, he proposed by mail to his future wife, Leva Grimes, and then brought her from Illinois to Las Vegas. They built the well-known Beckley House at 120 Fourth Street for $2,500, in the popular California Bungalow Style, which fared better than many other types in a desert environment. At that time, Will Beckley moved his business to the old Nevada Hotel, which advantageously faced the railroad depot. Together, the Beckley couple contributed to the Las Vegas community: he by offering a fair deal and quality goods to the citizens and visitors, and she by bringing gracious living to the dusty small community. She was a charter member of the Mesquite Club and was instrumental in establishing most of the social and cultural organizations in Las Vegas. Their home was also truly a center for social activity. Although death took her husband in 1965, Leva Beckley remained there until 1978 when ill health forced her to move in with family members at age 93. Fortunately, the house was not a victim of the wrecking ball, as so many other historical homes and businesses were. Through the efforts of the Junior League, the house now stands on Heritage Street at the Clark County Museum.

As the town's fortunes rose and fell over the years, so did those of the Von Tobel Lumberyard. Once the town was built, the need for lumber declined and Von Tobel managed to buy out two of his competitors. Then during another low period, he bought out his partner Beckley, who ended up working in his own brother's clothing store. In 1908, Von Tobel married a Bavarian woman who bore him three sons and a daughter over the next decade. Through good times and bad, Ed Von Tobel never gave up on Las Vegas. He would make the city his home until his death at age 92, leaving a legacy of construction and real estate development unmatched by his peers. He may not have shared Mayor Buol's incurable optimism, but he did evidence another quality that would always be essential to success in Las Vegas: tenacity.

Most certainly, that's what it took to thrive in the townsite in those early years. Women, in particular, were put to hardship by the local environment. Dust, heat, dryness, solar radiation, strong winds, flash floods, foul odors, mud, insects . . . these were not the living conditions the "fairer sex" preferred. Mayme Stocker, who arrived in Las Vegas in 1911, stated her first impression of the town quite bluntly: "Anybody who lives here is out of his mind." Years later, she would explain to a reporter for the *Las Vegas Review-Journal*, "There were no streets or sidewalks, and there were no flowers, lawns or trees." With no streetlights to light the way, a lantern had to be carried to walk downtown at night. "After a rain, the walk was unpleasant because of the puddles of water left in the street. Ground, which appeared to be firm by the light of a lantern, often turned out to be wet and slippery, a hazard to a woman wearing a long skirt."

Most of the women who lived in early Las Vegas had, like Helen Stewart, followed their men there. Cut off from the urban culture of the cities they were raised in, they banded together to form social groups. One such gathering was the Women's Civic League. Another was the Anti-Gaming League, which successfully pressured the Nevada legislature to outlaw all forms of gambling throughout the state in 1909. The open card games of Las Vegas saloons were thus forced to move behind closed doors for 20 years after promulgation of the new ordinance on October 1, 1910. By 1912, the women's rights movement had blossomed and the town was considered large enough to warrant stops by members of the National American Women's Suffrage Association (NAWSA), who visited Las Vegas by train, stagecoach, motor car, and horseback, campaigning for the right to vote.

But not all women in the Clark County seat sought community involvement. In fact, a certain group of them preferred to be ignored as much as possible by legal statutes and public scrutiny—the ladies of Block 16. Bounded by Stewart and Ogden, First and Second Streets, Block 16 was home to all of the city's bars and so-called "fancy houses," saloon-bordellos that featured "cribs" in the rear. The only other liquor-zoned section of Las Vegas, Block 17, turned out to be superfluous and gradually became the site for all the town's minority-held businesses. By 1906, Block 16 had already gained a reputation as the place for bawdy and rowdy entertainment. Passengers on the SPLA&SL discovered it was just close enough to the depot to allow for wetting their whistles during water stops. Not a few of those in transit missed their onward trains and stayed the night in Las Vegas with a red-light district companion.

Any visitor to Block 16 in those days would have had to be impressed by one building there—the luxurious Arizona Club. It was the best known of the businesses on Block 16. At the 1905 auction, J.C "Jim" McIntosh had purchased land for the club, intent on creating the town's swankiest establishment. With marble baseboards, beveled glass-inlaid doors, and an ornate, extremely long carved mahogany bar—reputed to have come from a Virginia City establishment, complete with bullet holes—the Arizona Club was the class of its competitors. Gas lights illuminated its interior, even after 1907 when electricity was introduced. Three pianists performed for its guests. Drinks, including the house special sloe-gin fizz, went for 15¢ a glass or two for a quarter. Nickel slot machines, faro, roulette, and blackjack kept the customers entertained, at least until the anti-gaming bill passed. It was not until 1912, when McIntosh sold out, that the Arizona Club went the way of its neighbors, becoming the first Las Vegas saloon to build a second story for the express reason of offering prostitution to please its patrons. The Queen of Block 16 would reign without challenge until 1941, providing employment and entertainment in equal measure.

Edward W. Griffith, an entrepreneur in his own right, who purchased two of the original townsite lots in May 1905, had some very different ideas about how to entertain people in Las Vegas. He opened the Majestic Theatre in 1912 to show motion pictures and stage vaudeville acts. Making use of space originally occupied by the Opera House, the Majestic replaced the town's first indoor movie house, the 1908 Isis Theatre, which had been razed for further expansion of the Las Vegas Club. Three years later, Griffith would open Mt. Charleston's first summer resort at Kyle Canyon.

During the hot summer months after World War I, Griffith's movies were shown at the Airdome, an outdoor theater on the northeast corner of Third and Fremont Streets set up by Ernie Cragin and William Pike. Children would often peek through the slats of the surrounding wooden fence to see a free show. When it rained, patrons would help the projectionist carry the equipment back to the Majestic. This arrangement served the movie-going interests of Las Vegas citizenry until 1928, when the glamorous and regal El Portal Theatre was opened on the grounds of the old Airdome. The El Portal's first movie was "Ladies of the Mob," starring Clara Bow. A year later, the venue would introduce "talkies" (movies with sound) to the Las Vegas public. The theater was to be the scene of many special premieres throughout the years, especially the debut of films having to do with Las Vegas itself, delighting the city with the era's favorite medium for culture, news, and entertainment.

In like fashion, John F. Miller, who purchased the property at 1 Main Street across from the railroad station in 1905, sought to bring a bit of comfort and style to Las Vegas lodgings. Miller erected a small stone building that was palatial compared to the surrounding tents and other rudimentary hotels that had sprung up. It was called the Hotel Nevada and is most likely the oldest structure still remaining on Fremont Street. In 1906, it was described as being "first-class" and "as comfortable a hostelry as can be found anywhere, with large rooms (10' x 10'), electric lighting, ventilation and steam heat radiators." Las Vegas's first telephone was installed here. The phone number? "Ring '1,' please."

Although the serving of alcoholic beverages had been restricted from the very beginning to Blocks 16 and 17, John Wisner, the owner of Main Street's Overland Hotel, flaunted the regulations and opened a saloon, which the rail company tried unsuccessfully to shut down. In response, the Hotel Nevada served up iced beverages of its own that attracted a fair share of local clientele seeking escape from the burning rays of the afternoon sun. Along with Squires's canvas-topped Hotel Las Vegas just to the north, the hotels of Main Street soon became the center of the town's social activity.

Destiny's Water Stop

For cooling off outdoors, the first popular place to swim was the Las Vegas Ranch, which eventually saw its water supply change from a simple creek to a dammed reservoir, and then a concrete pool. The ranch operated as a true ranch, continuing to grow and sell produce, and also as an early resort, with tent cabins for overnight guests. Besides swimming, there was often dancing in the evening. An early attempt was made to show movies there as well, but that idea never quite caught on.

Another popular place to swim in the 1920s was the Plunge at well-shaded Ladd's resort near 12th Street, developed by James Ladd, one of the city's earliest hotel creators. Closer to the commercial and heavily-developed residential areas was the Mermaid Pool on Fifth Street just north of Fremont. It was considered somewhat elite because it was completely surrounded with a high fence. Although Block 16 may have given Las Vegas its initial image as a hard-drinking, gun-toting frontier town, the seeds of civilized culture had been planted in dozens of other blocks around the townsite. Suits were replacing chaps; horses were making way for motors cars. From 1925, Fremont Street was paved between Main and Fifth Streets.

Another man who developed a vision for local social life was a young European artistocrat and second cousin to the King of Monaco, David G. Lorenzi. He was a relative late-comer to Las Vegas, arriving in 1911, but he soon became the forerunner of the city's great resort-makers. Attracted to the valley by reports of untapped artesian wells beneath the desert floor, Lorenzi purchased 80 acres of land 2 miles from the railroad tracks and immediately began digging for water. He hoped to grow grapes that could be made into wine equal to that produced in his native country, France. As he envisioned, the fruit grew and the wine it yielded was good. But unfortunately, Vegas was still a beer and whisky town. Without a local market, the vintner's business never took off.

Undaunted, Lorenzi married Julia Traverse Moore in 1913 and they opened a downtown parlor called The Palms, serving ice cream, fresh fruit, and homemade candy. Using the soon-successful confectionery as a base, together they then undertook a project much more ambitious than farming or shopkeeping—to turn the irrigation ditches of the failed vineyard into a true desert oasis. Over the next dozen years, two artificial lakes would be dug, filled with fresh water 10 feet deep and covering more than 3 acres. Each one would sport its own island connected to the shore by bridges. One island featured a band shell for movies and concerts; the other offered a "social building" for discrete card games and unfettered consumption of alcohol.

The Lorenzi Resort, also known as Twin Lakes, opened to the public in May 1928. Its Independence Day celebration that year featured fireworks, bathing beauties, and even a parachutist, attracting a stream of revelers that reportedly clogged the road all the way in from downtown Las Vegas. The owners would later add other attractions, from prize-fighting and horse races, to dance contests and beauty pageants. Charging visitors just 10¢ for use of all facilities, the resort included Nevada's largest swimming pool, a fleet of rowboats, and riding stables. Lloyd St. John and his son Richard would acquire the property in 1947 and give it a new name: Twin Lakes Lodge. It had a 48-room motel and became a complete dude ranch for celebrity divorcees awaiting their six-weeks residency requirement. Lorenzi himself would die three years before his final wish of seeing the land become a city park was realized in 1965. Today, the acreage bears his name, Lorenzi Park, and is home to wildlife, a community center for seniors that occupies some of the original motel buildings, and the Nevada State Museum and Historical Society.

Amazingly, perhaps, Las Vegas managed to escape some of the worst aspects of the early twentieth century. World War I may have claimed the lives of a few city relatives, but the faraway European conflict had little impact on the southern Nevada community as a whole. The Spanish Flu Epidemic, which claimed millions of lives worldwide in 1918 and 1919, scarcely caused a sneeze in Las Vegas, although it killed many in the more humid regions upstate. Even the enforcement of the Volstead Act, prohibiting the production, sale, and consumption of alcohol, despite President Woodrow Wilson's veto in 1919, did little to slow free-wheeling Las Vegas. Under Prohibition, bootleggers and speakeasies proliferated. North of the city limits, huge basements with distillery equipment were located beneath new houses and it was said that some of the establishments had underground tunnels leading from one bar to another.

That is not to say the community ignored the rule of law—not completely. When Lincoln County was divided in 1909, newly created Clark County elected its first sheriff. That position would be filled by a no-nonsense peace officer named Charles C. Corkhill. It was the sheriff's strong and free-minded 49-year-old deputy, however, who would become the best-remembered lawman in Las Vegas history.

Sam Gay was a giant of a man, 6 feet tall and weighing between 245 and 260 pounds. His boots were size 13. A Canadian by birth, Gay grew up in Massachusetts and came west to seek his fortune, first in California and then in Alaska during its gold rush of 1900. By 1902, he had drifted to Nevada, swinging a pick axe in the mining town of Goldfield, where he heard of opportunities in Las Vegas, the next "happening" town in the West.

Making the most of his size, Gay was able to get a job as a bouncer at Jim McIntosh's Arizona Club in 1905. He did not wear a gun, but his heavy fists and quick boots did the job of keeping peace in the bustling saloon. When a fight would break out between customers, Gay would grab the hooligans by their necks, take them into the street, and bang their heads together until they settled down. If they turned out to be particularly uncooperative, he would tie them up and hose them down until they cooled off.

Despite his frequent use of force, Gay was known as a fair and compassionate man, a reputation which won him appointment as the Las Vegas night watchman in January 1906, followed by election to the post of town constable later in the year. In 1908, Lincoln County Sheriff Orrin K. Smith chose "Big Sam" to be his deputy for the southern region. When the division came, Gay was the natural choice for deputy sheriff of the new county. Two years later, he would unseat his boss and himself become the Clark County sheriff, a title he would keep until late 1930.

As the region's top cop, Sam Gay brought his own ideas about law enforcement to bear, often resorting to some rather unorthodox methods. For example, he would summarily kick vagrants and misdemeanor suspects out of town without trial, claiming that it saved the county court and jail costs while ensuring that offenders would avoid his jurisdiction in the future. To law-abiding folks, Gay was friendly and respectful. To troublemakers, he could be a terror. Yet, when temperatures soared inside the cramped county jail known as the Blue Room, Gay might take his prisoners outside and chain them to shade trees—sometimes leaving them there overnight. He could be compassionate—if only to a degree—with criminals and he could be quite clever, too. During the tension-packed rail strike of 1922, the sheriff sided with the workers and deputized several of them to keep things calm—a peacekeeping ploy that worked surprisingly well.

Sam Gay's two-decade reign as sheriff did not pass without incident, however. Accused by local District Attorney Albert Henderson of "gross intoxication" in 1915—after the sheriff had playfully shot out the electric lights along Fremont Street one night—Gay had to swear off booze for as long as he continued to hold office. Prohibition in 1919 may have helped him keep that promise, but he refused to enforce anti-drinking laws that he considered foolish. He felt the same way about the state's anti-gambling ordinance and turned a blind eye to the back rooms of Las Vegas saloons.

For a brief time in 1917, the mighty sheriff seemed to have met his match when he was suspended for protecting a deputy who had a run-in with Justice of the Peace William Harkins. But as fate would have it, Gay was so popular he was easily reelected in 1918 . . . and every four years thereafter until, at the ripe age of 70, he decided to let his previously-maligned deputy, Joe Keate, take the reins. Sam Gay's death in 1932 drew a record number of mourners. He was buried with a solid gold badge given to him, "Compliments of Las Vegas Friends."

During Sam Gay's life in Las Vegas, he had witnessed the passing of one significant milestone after another. He had seen the original ancestors of the neon that would define Glitter Gulch, as the first electric lights were installed along Fremont Street in 1907, powered by a single-cylinder, 90-horsepower generator dubbed "old Betsy." In 1909, he had browsed a newly published weekly named the *Clark County Review*, predecessor to the 1929 *Las Vegas Review* and eventually today's *Las Vegas Review-Journal*. He had stood by the railway tracks in 1911 as city residents waved hello to William Howard Taft, the first President to pass through Las Vegas. And the following year, he had greeted to office another important president, local businessman James Givens, who presided over the newly opened Las Vegas Chamber of Commerce.

Unknown to Gay or anyone else at the time, that strike he had helped control in 1922 was symptomatic of a turning point in history. The glorious age of America's railroads had peaked. The strike was preceded by William Clark's sale of his rail interests to an old rival, the Union Pacific, in 1921. If the SPLA&SL had run Las Vegas like a company store, at least its vision for the city's future had been clear. Under Union Pacific management, conditions took a turn for the worse. Fearful of the future, local railroad employees joined a nationwide walk-out of 400,000 workers. When the strike was settled, the Union Pacific punitively closed the Las Vegas repair shops and moved its maintenance base to Caliente, eliminating jobs and sending residents packing.

Without the support of the railroad, upon which the city seemed so dependent for everything, the future must have appeared bleak indeed. But several changes were coming to Las Vegas, not the least of which was the arrival of air travel. The city's first airport, Anderson Field, was completed in 1921, approximately where the Sahara Hotel's auxiliary parking lot is now located, on the southeast corner of Sahara and Paradise. Coincidentally, the opening of the air field meant there was now an alternative to long train rides for far-off visitors to access two newly created tourist attractions in the vicinity: Grand Canyon National Park in Arizona and Zion National Park in Utah, established by acts of Congress only two years earlier.

In late 1925, the air facility was renamed Rockwell Field when the land was acquired by the Rockwell brothers, Leon and Earl. The city's first airmail service was then inaugurated by Western Air Express (WAE) on April 17, 1926 and passenger air service began soon after at advertised rates of $45 from Los Angeles to Las Vegas, or $80 round trip. Operating at least one flight daily in its first year of operation, WAE could carry 41 paying passengers in addition to cargo. The first of those was A.B. DeNault, vice president of the Piggly Wiggly chain of grocery stores. Visiting VIPs by the hundreds would soon follow. By 1929, the air field had outgrown its location and was moved to the area where Nellis Air Force Base now stands. Placement of Las Vegas on the nation's air routes was initially strategic—the city's location made it a perfect refueling depot for the burgeoning aviation industry. And what a hub it would become!

The 1920 census showed 2,304 residents in Las Vegas. That number would more than double by the end of the decade, including significant increases in the city's ethnic minorities who had been confined, for the most part, to Block 17. In an effort to explain this segregation, Walter Bracken had written in 1911:

> Our colored population, Mexicans, etc., is growing rapidly and unless we
> have some place for this class of people they will be scattered through our
> town. You will notice in my pricing of lots that I have made the prices of lots
> in 17 such that they can be picked up by the above described classes. Blocks
> 16 and 17 are designated "Red Light" districts but there is no likelihood of

17 ever being used for this purpose or even the East half of Block 16 as the saloons are complying with the Hotel law and spreading all over town and it would make little difference to colored people and foreigners about living so close to the Red Light District. We of course could not herd these classes of people to any certain block, but it seems to be their desire to get down in that part of town, and other property owners in town are refusing to sell them property where they will be mixed up with white people.

Bracken's discrimination did not stop one homeowner of Mexican descent, Mary Marino, and her daughter Frances from setting up residence on Main Street before the town incorporated, but the Marinos may have been the exception that proved the rule. For the most part, Hispanics drifted in and out of the community, picking up wages as rail workers, stable-keepers, and farm laborers, then moving on to other locations. Among those who stayed, a Mexican man established the successful Spanish Restaurant in 1909 and a Mexican woman purchased the Cochran Beauty Business in 1913. By 1914, the number of Mexicans living in Clark County reached into the hundreds, enough of them resident in Las Vegas to warrant a big celebration on Mexican Independence Day.

Under the direction of Tomas Perea, D. Pecetto, and A.G. Gonzales, a gala ball was held at the Union Hotel on First and Bridger on September 16. Angel Lopez served as floor manager, decorating the room in bunting of red, white, and blue as well as red, white, and green. Many of the community's non-Hispanics were invited to join in the festivities, which Pop Squires reported in his *Las Vegas Age* newspaper. The party ran well into the night, with a musical and literary program, plenty of Mexican food, and dancing to tunes provided by a live orchestra. By all accounts, it was a lively affair, with a cordial multiracial and bicultural atmosphere.

"Tolerance" best describes the general attitude of Las Vegas's white population toward its minorities in the first two decades of cityhood. They might not have mixed much socially, but it was quite common for the races to do business with each other. Indeed, local white-owned enterprises openly invited trade with African-American, Hispanic, and Asian customers, welcoming them to most of the city's shops, restaurants, and places of entertainment. The only obvious exception was the fancy houses of Block 16, which were strictly off limits to non-whites. Recognizing an opportunity, saloon-keepers in Block 17 quickly established brothels of their own and segregation of sexual services never became an issue.

Although blatant racism was not yet apparent, discrimination already existed to some degree in the local job market, with the best jobs going to people of European heritage. The railroad was a major employer of all races, of course, but its wage scales favored Italian and Irish Americans, for example, over their African- and Asian-

American counterparts. In time, arrivals from the nation's "Jim Crow" southern states would bring their racial prejudices with them to the community and storm clouds would appear in the atmosphere of tolerance. Almost as a harbinger of confrontations to come, the NAACP established a presence in Las Vegas in 1928 and questions of civil rights were raised for the first time on the local level.

Ironically, the two groups of people who had given the valley its first communities were conspicuously absent from the early affairs of Las Vegas: the Mormons and the local Native Americans. Church guidelines advised the Latter-Day Saints (LDS) against land speculation, so their members avoided the railroad's townsite auction of 1905. Only slowly would they return to the area. One notable Mormon resident was Charles C. Ronnow, a former bishop from the LDS enclave in Panaca, Nevada, who became a co-owner in the Clark Forwarding Company. Another prominent Mormon, Newell K. Leavitt, would come to work for Ronnow in 1913 and start a Sunday school in the living room of his Sixth and Bridger home. Gradually, other members of the church followed, so that by 1925, Ira J. Earl was named first bishop of the First Ward of Las Vegas, which counted within its precincts 175 members and a brand-new, gleaming white wood-frame chapel on the corner of Sixth and Carson. Earl would be succeeded as bishop in 1929 by Edward Bunker Sr., who would in turn go on to become the president of the Salt Lake Temple.

The Southern Paiute, meanwhile, had seen their numbers dwindle year by year. The settlers had taken over the best land, blocked access to water, and restricted their movements. The railroad was at once a source of jobs and a destroyer of their way of life. Mindful of the tribe's predicament, on December 30, 1911, Helen Stewart deeded ten of her remaining acres on the old Las Vegas Ranch "for the use of the Paiute Indians." The section would be bought by the federal government for $500 and titled to the tribe as Las Vegas Colony land on April 17, 1912.

Thereafter, the Las Vegas Paiute would have a permanent home, but their troubles were far from over. The new reservation provided no system of formal education for their 35 school-aged children, no easily obtained water, and no proper sewerage. Tuberculosis took the lives of many. Plagued by health problems and pressure from the growing city, the Native Americans told their federal supervisor in 1913 that they "would soon pass away and leave their homes to the whites" if assistance could not be provided. The bureaucrat's response was a shocker: relocate to a larger reservation in Moapa, Nevada.

No tribal debate was necessary. Abandoning their age-old home in the Las Vegas Valley was simply out of the question. For the next five years, nothing happened. Then, in 1918, Indian Affairs Superintendent L.B. Sandall—a thin man whom the Native Americans called "Mosquito Legs"—declared the Las Vegas Colony inadequate and closed the local branch of the Southeast Nevada Indian Agency. The Paiute were left on their own.

If the arrival of the Iron Horse had nearly caused the demise of the Las Vegas tribe, could the railroad's own end spur their revival? In October 1918, operations ceased on the unprofitable Las Vegas and Tonopah rail branch. The tracks were torn up the following year and the land sold for $4,000 to the Nevada Highway Department for development of a graded road. The age of the automobile was dawning. Foreseeing the importance of motorcar traffic to the Las Vegas economy, the city's leaders had already drawn $10,000 from municipal funds in 1914 to improve the road southwest to Jean, Nevada, in the direction of California. Bonds were then sold in 1918 to raise $75,000 for improvement of the thoroughfare that would one day become Interstate 15, connecting Las Vegas to Los Angeles and Salt Lake City.

As motorists began to discover Las Vegas and the town continued to grow into the next decade, the Southern Paiute learned to survive by selling handcrafted baskets to tourists. Although it could take nearly a year to weave a single large basket, which would sell for just $3 or $4, the income from two or three baskets could buy shoes for a Native American child and the crafts could sometimes be traded for groceries or clothing.

Until the late 1920s, young Las Vegas Native American children had to be sent to the boarding school at Fort Mohave for their studies. Many of them spent years there, unable to return to their homes. Isolated from their parents, they lost touch with the traditional values and customs of the Southern Paiute people. Speaking their own dialect at school could result in a mouth-washing with soap. Leg-irons and whippings awaited those who broke the fort's strict rules or attempted to run away.

Back on the reservation, conditions were not much better for Native American adults. A 1926 report described 50 tribe members using the 10-acre colony as their base:

> . . . some living there permanently. They have no tillable land and are all self supporting by labor in and around Las Vegas, the women washing and doing domestic work; the men doing ordinary labor by the day on the ranches. All the Indians in the surrounding country who visit this section make this small Reservation their headquarters, thus giving this small Reservation a very fluctuating population.

Those were tough times for a once proud and free people, but soon their life of hardship would be shared by almost everyone in the country. In October 1929, the stock market crashed, signaling the start of the Great Depression.

Chapter Three

CURES FOR A DECADE OF DEPRESSION

Even before the 1929 collapse of the stock market, Las Vegas was beginning to encounter some major difficulties. Removal of the railroad maintenance shops by the Union Pacific affected much of the city's populace, but a more fundamental problem threatened everyone's survival: the abundant water that had drawn early settlers to "The Meadows" was now becoming seriously depleted. As the valley's population more than doubled between 1910 and 1920, then redoubled by 1930, the supply of water could hardly keep pace with demand. The output of once gushing artesian wells was beginning to slow to a trickle.

Not surprisingly, rumors of a dam to be built on the Colorado River brought excitement and new hope to Las Vegans. This idea had actually been in the works for some time, with several hits and misses. In fact, as early as 1904, discussion had begun about taming the wild Rio Grande, which had frequently caused destructive floods throughout the Southwest. In 1905, a particularly damaging flood caused California's Imperial Valley to fill with water, forming the Salton Sea. Two years of dredging and levee-building were required to close the break and return the river to its main channel. Estimated costs and property losses ran into millions of dollars.

By 1919, the talk started getting serious. Damming the river could avert future calamities, make drinking and irrigation water available, and allow the generation of hydroelectric power. The United States Bureau of Reclamation had looked at 70 potential sites for a dam and was considering two major canyons, both near Las Vegas, as prospective locations: Boulder Canyon and Black Canyon. Teams of specialists spent a year methodically examining and evaluating the two areas. One preliminary team was headed up by Arthur Powell Davis, director of the reclamation service, who had a long history of supervising the design and construction of an extensive list of dams, tunnels, and irrigation canals. Notably, Davis was the nephew of John Wesley Powell, a celebrated nineteenth-century explorer of the Colorado River. It had been Davis's dream to grow up and harness the river's power.

First impressions indicated that Boulder Canyon was the more preferable of the two sites. Not only Nevadans, but also federal officials soon took to calling the project Boulder Dam. However, after a year of further testing under sometimes harrowing conditions, Black Canyon was designated the final site. Apart from its desirable rock formations, it could be served by a shorter rail line than Boulder Canyon, which meant big savings in the construction budget.

In 1923, Davis proposed a dam "at or near" Boulder Canyon; hence, when the actual bill was submitted in 1928 by California congressmen Philip Swing and Hiram Johnson, it was called the Boulder Canyon Act. It would take another two years for the plan authorized by President Calvin Coolidge to become a reality—with appropriations coming from Congress on December 30, 1930—but when the signing of the Swing-Johnson Bill was announced on December 21, 1928, the people of Las Vegas went wild. Land prices soared almost immediately as residents realized that this meant a huge change in their economy. There would be an influx of people from all over the country to help build the dam, which in turn would mean more business for the city of Las Vegas.

The winning bid for construction of the dam and its power plant was submitted in March 1931 by a consortium of major western contracting firms called Six Companies, Inc., including the involvement of Henry J. Kaiser and W.A. Bechtel Company, among others. At an estimated cost of $48,890,995, it would be the largest engineering project undertaken in the Western Hemisphere since the Panama Canal. Cement plants, gravel depots, power and telegraph lines, roads, water mains, and housing were needed. Getting construction material to the dam site alone would require the laying of 52 miles of special railroad tracks, roughly half of it built by the Union Pacific from its main line to a town site originally called Summit, then later renamed Boulder City. Completed at incredible speed, by late April the new branch line opened and regular train service commenced between Las Vegas and the project.

On May 26, 1931, the plat and description of the Boulder Canyon Project Federal Reservation reached the office of Nevada governor Fred Balzar in Carson City. The land to be appropriated in Clark County would cover 144 square miles, including the dam and town sites, as well as a considerable tract of open territory around what would become Boulder City. Acceptance of the plan by Balzar formally established federal jurisdiction and the Boulder Dam Project was officially underway.

Originally, many Nevadans assumed that the dam site workers would be housed in Las Vegas, but Commissioner of Reclamation Elwood Mead and Interior Secretary Raymond Lyman Wilbur had long known otherwise. They had visited the Clark County seat in June 1929. Despite attempts to clean up the town for their visit—city officials going so far as to close Block 16 temporarily and erect an arch over Fremont Street, proclaiming Las Vegas as the Gateway to Boulder Dam—the plan had always been to construct a government town on land close to the construction site. On the federal reservation, order and morality would prevail. There would be "no liquor, no gambling or other practices deemed injurious to the workers." Boulder City would become "a wholesome American community."

Some Las Vegans took affront to the federal government's branding of their city as a "boisterous frontier town" unsuited to hosting the work crews. Their bitterness was short-lived, however, as they realized how the dam's millions of dollars of supplies would be shipped and stored locally even if the employees were not resident there. What's more, if the new federal reservation of Boulder City would not allow "wine, women and song" (a euphemism for alcohol, prostitutes, and gambling), the workers would simply have to seek all of that in Las Vegas on their days off.

One small business that profited from the flow of laborers was a restaurant called the Green Shack. Originally located near Boulder Dam, it had opened in 1930 under the name Colorado. A California woman, "Jimmie" Jones, bought the green building from the railroad, then renamed and relocated it on Fremont Street. Some of the tables of the Green Shack were obtained from the Boulder Dam cafeteria. Jones's customers were construction workers from the dam, who followed her to the new venue to partake of her homemade fried chicken and bootleg whiskey. Two years after the move, the restaurant was purchased by the McCormick family, who managed it for the next six decades. In 1994, the well-known green building was listed on the National Register of Historical Places, but it closed permanently in 1999, leaving its future very much in question. Official designation, unfortunately, does not ensure protection of a property or keep it from being torn down.

In 1930, 40 new buildings were planned by Las Vegas developers in anticipation of the impending boom. Consolidated Power and Telephone, the area's primary utility, split into two companies—Southern Nevada Power and Southern Nevada Telephone—which quickly began implementing plans to expand their networks, including the introduction of long-distance telephone service. In short order, the city commission implemented one improvement after another. New streetlights were installed, new sanitation trucks were purchased, the police force was expanded, and the city's first zoning ordinance went into effect. To pave, widen, and extend existing city streets, bonds were issued in 1931, raising $165,000 in construction funds. In conjunction with the road improvements, federal monies were tapped to connect Fremont Street by road to the dam site—a thoroughfare that would later become Boulder Highway. Similarly, $150,000 in bond funds were obtained to extend the old 1911 sewer system to newer neighborhoods. The modernization of Las Vegas from frontier town to full-fledged city was underway.

Among the many improvements seen in Las Vegas upon the advent of the Boulder Dam project was the opening of the community's first real hospital. Until 1931, medical care had been provided by private physicians, such as Dr. Roy Martin, who along with his associates Dr. Forrest Mildren and Dr. F.M. Ferguson had operated a 12-bed clinic on the second floor of the Palace Hotel since 1917. The Missouri-educated Dr. Martin had come to Las Vegas in August following Clark's townsite auction of 1905, en route to the mining districts of Rhyolite, Nevada. Folklore has it that a disgruntled Las Vegas physician offered to sell Martin his local practice, equipment and all, for the $10 fare to Los Angeles. Martin didn't have the money, but he allegedly challenged the town's fastest sprinter to a foot race, which the young doctor won, earning the funds needed to buy out his predecessor. Thereafter, he served as chief surgeon for the Las Vegas and Tonopah Railroad, traveling far and wide to attend to patients. In June 1906, he set up an office in the Thomas Building on First and Fremont Streets, which included a pharmacy as well as 12 beds.

Early in 1931, Drs. Martin and Ferguson decided that the city was ready for a truly first-class medical facility. Together with a third partner, Dr. R.D. Balcum, they formed the Las Vegas Hospital Association and they had acquired land at the corner of Eighth and Ogden by April. For a total investment of $100,000, they began construction of a two-story, gypsum-block building with 35 beds and state-of-the-art facilities, such as an X-ray machine and special lighting for the operating room. The Las Vegas Hospital opened its doors in December 1931 and, although the original building was destroyed by fire in 1988, it was the forerunner of what is today known as University Medical Center (UMC), one of the nation's top 100 medical facilities.

At the same time as this upgrading of local healthcare services, the city's educational program was undergoing its own transformation. Overseeing this development was Maude Frazier, superintendent of the Las Vegas School Union District, which included two elementary schools as well as a high school built in 1910 that had recently been razed by fire. Frazier was a pioneering woman in all senses. She had come to Las Vegas from Nevada's mining country, where she had learned to ride horses, and taught classes in tents and brothels converted to schoolhouses. In the town of Genoa in 1906, she had become one of the state's first female principals. Fifteen years later, the 6-foot-tall, 40-year-old educator was appointed by the state department of education as deputy superintendent for all schools in Esmerelda, Nye, Lincoln, and Clark Counties. The assignment brought her to Las Vegas in 1921 and, six years later, to her position as the city's top educator, a post she would hold for 18 years.

In 1929, Frazier convinced the city commission to issue school bonds and allocate a $350,000 building fund to replace the fire-damaged secondary school. Many decried such a huge outlay for "rooms that will never be used," but the superintendent's will was unshakable. Her vision was to create a model high school that could serve the needs of students throughout Clark County. It would be an architecturally-distinct structure, a place to be admired inside and out. The new Las Vegas High School opened in 1930 with Maude Frazier serving as its principal. The building—a unique and beautiful Art Deco edifice, now home to Las Vegas Academy—today appears on the National Register of Historical Places, one of 35 Clark County sites so listed, including the Fifth Street School and the post office and federal building opened in 1933.

Not every endeavor during the city's dam-inspired growth period went smoothly. In 1930, for example, J.M. Heaton launched Las Vegas onto the air waves by establishing

Radio KGIX, but advertising dollars were harder to come by than expected and the station ultimately failed. The cost of so many infrastructure improvements all but depleted the coffers of the municipal and county governments. Power outages were common as demand for electricity outstripped capacity. Local financial institutions were suspect in the wake of bank collapses elsewhere in the state. And the presence of federal officials made life increasingly difficult for Las Vegas bootleggers, who had boldly defied Prohibition in isolation from government scrutiny until work on the dam began. In February 1931, federal agents staged their first major raid on Las Vegas speakeasies, followed in May by the arrest of over 100 persons, including policemen as well as bootleggers. Seized by the agents were 233 gallons of whiskey, 3 gallons of gin, and 15 gallons of beer. Nearly three dozen people were arraigned on federal charges. It was a thirsty summer that followed—which was exactly what the governing architects of Boulder Dam wanted.

Up in Boulder City, a strict manager was overseeing the development of the new community of workers: an "honest, upright, thoughtful" man named Sims Ely. His town was built to government specifications. His powers were practically absolute. Even the local police reported directly to Ely. Although the Bureau of Reclamation appointed a three-man committee to advise him, they had no authority over the Tennessee-born autocrat. Ely personally approved or denied all business permits. He was the superintendent of local grammar schools until 1933. He decided who would work or not work on the dam. He alone determined who could live in Boulder City. When he decreed in December 1932 that drunkenness would be cause for dismissal and expulsion, no one dared challenge him. The sale of alcoholic beverages in Boulder City would remain banned, not just until the repeal of Prohibition in 1933 or Ely's own retirement in 1941 at age 79, but—incredible as it may seem—until 1969.

Undoubtedly, Ely's obsessive control of the Boulder City population of 5,000 made it possible for Las Vegas to profit from the dam workers' unmet desires. His firmness and moral standards stood in stark contrast to those of the Las Vegas authorities. In 1930, then-mayor Fred Hesse was himself arrested for violating the Volsted Act. He wisely decided not to run for reelection in 1931, which paved the way for insurance man Ernie W. Cragin, who concurrently owned the El Portal Theatre, to capture the top office in a landslide victory. He would serve a popular ten years on and off, pressing for reforms that would make the city more attractive to tourists. Among those changes were paved sidewalks, increased speed limits (to 20 miles per hour), a new police station, new parking regulations, municipal swimming pools, and a city park.

It was on Cragin's watch, however, that racial discrimination grew. At his own cinema, he seated Hispanics and African Americans in separate sections from white patrons. He kept city funds from reaching the Westside, where ghetto conditions had been prevalent for two decades. Throughout the city, Mexican Americans were barred from casino jobs, denied bank loans, excluded from unions, and kept from entering certain swimming pools and dance halls. In the 1940s, Cragin would see that segregation was actively enforced throughout the city.

What eventually riled voters against Cragin was his cozy friendship with the head of the Southern Nevada Power (SNP). Whenever citizens complained about the supply or price of electricity, Cragin would side with SNP owner Ed Clark. In 1935, a relative newcomer to Las Vegas named Leonard Arnett, with the backing of local real estate developer John L. "Johnny" Russell, called for municipal ownership of the power company. This ploy was successful and Arnett ousted the incumbent mayor by a referendum vote of 2,117 to 215.

Cragin had to turn his attention (at least for the time being) to another way of promoting Las Vegas as a tourist destination; he became a key organizer of the Elks Club Helldorado Celebration. Inaugurated in April 1935, the week-long festival commemorated Old West gunslingers, prospectors, renegades, and pioneers and was the city's first attempt to attract visitors. Each year brought more festivities, including a rodeo and a "whiskering" event, in which the local men competed to see who could grow the thickest and longest beard in a designated period of time. By 1937, Helldorado, with its parades, fancy-dress costumes, high-spirited dances, and merrymaking entertainment, was well on its way to becoming a Las Vegas institution, inspiring cowboy star Tex Ritter to compose a hit song, "The Rodeo Boys," just for the occasion. In time, Western stars Roy Rogers and Dale Evans would publicize the event by making a movie using the celebration's title. Under censorship rules, however, the title was changed to "Heldorado."

With Cragin out of the way and an overwhelming mandate for change to back him, the new Las Vegas mayor should have been able to effect some big changes in local politics. As it happened, Arnett's take-over plans were thwarted by legal challenges thrown up by Clark and SNP. The power company remained in private hands. Then, in 1938, the progressive mayor disappeared on a 60-day leave of absence, reputedly for medical reasons, never to return to his job. Johnny Russell succeeded Arnett in 1939, but the local commissioners continued to block any attempts to take over local utilities. The political stalemate grew so bad that, for a short time in the early 1940s, Las Vegas operated under two city governments, each claiming the right to rule. Russell was eventually removed from office by a local court, which found him guilty of eight counts of malfeasance. Two weak governments followed, leading to the uncontested reelection of Ernie Cragin in 1943. The "old ways" eventually won out.

Regardless of Las Vegas political intrigues, construction of the mighty dam proceeded apace. Excavation of the tunnels for diversion of the Colorado River began in June 1931. Twenty-eight months later, the work would be completed. As over 3.2 million cubic yards of concrete were poured to a height of 727 feet, the river water gathered and began to rise, creating what would soon become Boulder Lake (renamed Lake Mead in February 1936 to honor the Reclamation Commissioner, Dr. Elwood Mead, who passed away earlier that year). The resulting structure would be bigger than the greatest pyramid in Egypt—equivalent to a 60-story building, 45 feet deep at the crest, 660 feet deep at the base, and 1,244 feet wide at its greatest span.

Although it would not officially be named Hoover Dam until rededicated by an act of Congress in 1947, long before it was even finished, the project on the Colorado River in Black Canyon known as Boulder Dam had already become associated with the president under whom its construction would take place: Herbert Clark Hoover. Even the Union Pacific, in early promotion materials, referred to its rail connection to the area as "The Hoover Dam Route." In 1932, the President made a radio address that attempted to convey the magnitude of the project to the American public, saying, "This dam is the greatest engineering work of its character ever attempted at the hand of Man. The waters of this great river, instead of being wasted in the sea, will now be brought into use by Man."

In an era when jobs were scarce, the dam represented not only a visionary engineering project, but a source of employment as well. There is little wonder why thousands of dam workers willingly submitted to Sims Ely's dictatorial authority, accepted low wages, braved summer temperatures of over 100 degrees Fahrenheit, and lived in two-story dormitories or prefabricated, surplus cottages from the 1932 Olympics, which had been shipped from Los Angeles to Boulder City. Conditions could be difficult, often life-threatening. For at least 96 workers, and perhaps as many as 117, construction of the dam would prove fatal. But contrary to popular myth, no worker was ever buried in its concrete walls. The sections poured were so small that anyone who fell only needed to stand up to get clear of the rising cement. On November 8, 1933, one man came close to being buried in a collapsing wall. Laborer W.A. Jameson was covered in debris. He died, but his body was recovered after 16 hours and sent to Rock Hill, North Carolina, where he was buried by his brother and sister. Otherwise, construction went smoothly from almost all points of view.

There was, however, one unforeseen drawback to the Boulder Dam Project: the unwanted migration of jobless workers to the Las Vegas area. Between 1928 and 1935, tens of thousands of young men descended on southern Nevada in search of rumored employment. Most failed to find the work they were looking for and many, shunned away by Las Vegas police as hobos, ended up penniless in "Old Town," 100 acres of lawless land just north of the town limits, which had been a haven for moonshiners since 1919.

The de facto mayor of Old Town was Tom Williams, a farmer who had sectioned off part of his 160-acre estate for the establishment of homesites and churches. He envisioned a community governed by religious law and free of civil authority. Not surprisingly, the Prohibition-era sale of lots attracted more bootleggers than clerics. By 1932, the area had been turned into a encampment of makeshift shacks, shelters formed of scrap lumber and mud, canvas tents, and a maze of underground tunnels used to hide illegal booze from snooping federal agents. In reference to the President who had "caused" such shantytowns to spring up across the country, the squatters called the place Hooverville.

Williams and the other four members of the Old Town council did their best to make the community livable for everyone during those years of economic hardship. Emanuel Church became the town's social center. Washington Grammar School was built to educate the local children. And to dispel the stigma of its derogatory nicknames, the town fathers temporarily renamed their community Vegas Verde (Green Meadows). Throughout the 1930s, the population of the northern suburb grew slowly, reaching 2,000 by 1941. Williams suffered a stroke and died in 1939, but not before Prohibition was repealed by the 21st Amendment in 1933. The moonshiners moved on and his town gained the name it goes by even today—North Las Vegas.

Meanwhile, to help pull the nation out the Depression, in 1933 President Franklin Delano Roosevelt set in motion a series of programs called the New Deal. It included a package of legislative and administrative reforms aimed at putting Americans back to work. Apart from job-creating infrastructure projects, the New Deal included social and economic measures to regulate banks, distribute funds to the jobless, raise agriculture prices, and set standards for wages and production for industry.

One such action that helped wealth and jobs flow into Nevada under the New Deal was the Silver Purchase Act of 1934, whereby Roosevelt ordered federal purchase of the United States' entire annual silver output. Sagging exports had caused silver prices to fall dramatically in prior years, to a low of 43¢ per ounce. The new presidential order pegged the price for domestic silver at 62.5¢ per ounce and it rose gradually to 77.57¢ by the time the act expired in 1937. That was exactly the kind of economic boost the Silver State and its mining workforce needed. Gradually, the inflow of money and jobs trickled down to non-mining towns like Las Vegas, too.

Another New Deal windfall for Las Vegas was the formation of a "reforestation army," which would later be known as the Civilian Conservation Corps (CCC) of the Works Progress Administration (WPA). Congressman James "the Colonel" Scrugham, Nevada's former governor (1923–1927), was instrumental in seeing that southern Nevada got jobs from the CCC in April 1933. The Colonel, a staunch Democrat and former Kentuckian who had earned his nickname as a lieutenant colonel in the Army Reserve during World War I, told Roosevelt of "the distressing condition of thousands of able-bodied men drawn to Las Vegas through hopes of obtaining employment on the Boulder Dam Project." Proclaiming that those men "cannot be allowed to starve," Scrugham convinced the President to increase from 200 to 1,000 the number of jobs made available at two CCC camps in the Las Vegas Valley, one located at Mt. Charleston and the other at Boulder City.

Indeed, it was good politics and a keen understanding of human nature that allowed Las Vegas to weather the darkest days of the decade of depression. A case in point was how Ed Clark, owner of the First National Bank of Nevada (FNBN) from 1926 to 1937, handled a typical financial crisis in the early 1930s. When Acting Governor Morley Griswold declared a two-week banking holiday on November 1, 1932, to stave off panic withdrawals at the Reno-based Wingfield banks, depositors throughout the state were infuriated and threatened to storm the vaults of their financial institutions. Rather than bolt the bank's doors in Las Vegas, Clark stacked his counters high with hundreds of thousands of dollars worth of paper money and coins, all under the watchful eye of an armed guard. He then allowed FNBN customers to come in one by one to see the piles of cash and the sign he had posted: "This is your money. It is safe." Shrewdly, the banker would allow money to be withdrawn to pay for food and bills, but he refused to allow anyone to close out an account.

It was a gamble that paid off for Clark. Such bravado not only ensured the survival of FNBN, but also won a huge contract for SNP. In 1937, SNP secured the right to be the first utility to distribute electricity from Boulder Dam. Over the next 16 years, Clark would be the sole supplier of power to a desert community whose thirst for neon and air-conditioning would soon be as unquenchable as its desire for pumped water.

Unfortunately, not everyone benefited equally from the New Deal in Las Vegas. In fact, one segment of the community had a particularly hard time here throughout the 1930s—the city's African-American population. Until the Great Depression, racial discrimination had not been a major issue in the Valley, partly because the non-white minority was still so small (only 58 African-American residents were reported in Clark County in 1930) and partly because local African Americans kept pretty much to themselves. They lived mainly in and around Block 17, between First and Fifth Streets, bounded on the north by Stewart and the south by Ogden. There was tolerance between local whites and blacks, if not outright friendship. Although non-whites were not allowed in brothels, certain sections of the El Portal Theatre, fraternal clubs like the Elks, and the congregation of the First Methodist Church, segregation was not really the norm and race hatred was nowhere apparent. In fact, attempts by the Ku Klux Klan to organize a chapter in the city had been suspended in the early 1920s for lack of white support.

But the loss of jobs that marked the Depression years hit the African-American population of Las Vegas hardest. Maids, janitors, railroad porters, and track crews were among the first to be laid off. In 1931, the Six Companies of the Boulder Dam Project adopted an unstated policy of "whites only" that kept many otherwise-qualified workers from obtaining lucrative jobs. What few openings were to be had among the local trades went to "Caucasians first."

Understandably, many African Americans moved away from Las Vegas in search of employment elsewhere. Others simply moved across the tracks to the Westside, the old McWilliams Townsite, which had degenerated into a ragtown ghetto of poor whites and a few Hispanics, where water, power, and sewerage were in short supply, but land values and housing costs were low. During the 1930s, the Westside enjoyed little of the prosperity brought by the construction of the dam. By adding restrictive clauses to property deeds, or by otherwise limiting the sale of housing or land in other parts of town to whites only, Las Vegas made sure that the Westside and Old Town were the only areas where minorities could live.

Unwilling to sit idly as discrimination began to grow, a small group of African-American Las Vegans banded together in May 1931 to form the Colored Citizens' Labor and Protective Association of Las Vegas. Their initial goal was to desegregate the dam project, which had totally banned Chinese and African-American workers. With assistance from the national headquarters of the NAACP and the American Bar Association (ABA), they seemed to be successful in July 1932 when the Six Companies agreed to hire ten African-American workers. Unfortunately, this turned out to be a token gesture. By 1936, the total number of individual African Americans ever employed in the construction of Boulder Dam had reached only 44, compared to more than 20,000 for their white counterparts.

The hard times got harder as African Americans were gradually excluded from more and more aspects of the community. The local Veterans of Foreign Wars post barred them in 1932. One black student, Percy Powell, managed to graduate from Las Vegas High School in the 1930s, but segregation in the elementary schools soon became the norm. Unwanted in white political circles, the city's African Americans were forced to form their own Republican and Democratic Party clubs. Eventually, even the downtown casinos, which had always welcomed black patronage, began to close their gaming tables and bars to non-whites, ostensibly under pressure from tourists, who carried their racism with them from the deep south. Perhaps the only saving grace in the 1930s for African-American Las Vegans was the lack of other minorities to compete for the hotel jobs that started increasing in the latter part of the decade: maintenance, housekeeping, kitchen help, and groundskeeping.

During this difficult decade, the valley's indigenous people fared better, if only slightly. In Cedar City, Utah, the government agency responsible for the welfare of all Paiute reservations in the Southwest finally turned its attention to the Las Vegas Colony. The construction of Boulder Dam had made the city a tourist destination and interest in local Native American culture was rekindled to some degree. Submitting a petition to the Bureau of Indian Affairs (BIA), the Las Vegas tribe of Southern Paiute requested that improvements be made to their colony. This resulted in elaborate plans for beautification and new housing, but it turned out there was no money to implement them. The BIA could only find funds sufficient to build a windmill that pumped water into a small reservoir. Thankful for at least that small start, tribal leaders Harry Spute and Raymond Anderson decided to take matters into their own hands from there. They borrowed a team of horses from the Moapa Reservation, which they used to clear some colony land for gardens and to dig irrigation ditches. These improvements by no means compared to the prosperity seen elsewhere in the city, but the tribe appreciated what assistance it received. The new water supply and crops would allow the colony to live in self-sufficiency, at least until the middle of the next decade.

On May 29, 1935, the final bucket of concrete was poured, completing the great dam. Against the rosiest of expectations, the project had been brought in earlier than expected and under budget. On September 30, President Franklin Roosevelt presided over a dedication that officially proclaimed Boulder Dam finished. Its walls restrained the waters of the world's largest reservoir, and its electricity generators, which would whirl into action on October 26, 1936, would eventually supply over 1.8 million horsepower—the world's highest capacity.

Completion of the dam in 1936 meant an end to government-driven prosperity for Las Vegas. Jobs quickly evaporated and the dam workers left with them. But the city had a couple of "aces in the hole" to avoid a post-dam economic relapse. One of those was a state law enacted on May 1, 1931, that reduced the residence period required prior to divorce from three months to six weeks. In other states, long waiting periods for marriage and divorce were becoming common. Lawmakers took the institution of marriage seriously and wanted it to be difficult to enter into and dissolve. California, for example, had enacted a one-year waiting period preceding a final divorce decree and the right to remarry. Nevada's looser regulations for marriage and divorce attracted couples from all over the country seeking to get into or out of spousal relationships.

Although Reno was the city that most benefited from the shorter residence requirement, having already established itself as "The Divorce Capital of the World" in the opening decades of the twentieth century, Las Vegas lawyers and the courthouse soon saw an influx of divorce-minded visitors. Local businesses quickly discovered there was money to be made in serving these new temporary residents. Celebrity hook-ups and break-ups also helped put Las Vegas in the nation's headlines, the most notable being the "secret" wedding of film stars Clara Bow (the famous "It Girl") and Rex Bell (a cowboy idol and later lieutenant governor of Nevada) on December 3, 1931, and the highly publicized divorce of Clark Gable and his second wife Ria Franklin Langham on March 7, 1939. Indeed, the Las Vegas Chamber of Commerce sent photos and press releases to newspapers across the country, playing upon the nation's appetite for scandalous reports of Gable's dalliances with actress Carole Lombard in Hollywood while his estranged spouse lived it up throwing dice on Fremont Street, yachting on Lake Mead, and horseback riding in the open desert while waiting out her six mandatory weeks. Anticipating a surge of divorce-seekers in the months following all the publicity, a group of investors renovated the old Kyle Ranch north of town and renamed it the Boulderado Dude Ranch, the city's first haven created exclusively for prospective divorcees. That year, the number of divorces filed at the Clark County seat reached 738 and it would soon climb over 1,000.

For as much business as weddings and divorces would bring to Las Vegas, another "ace" dealt to the city by Nevada legislators in March 1931 would trump all others— the legalization of gambling. Oddly, the state's repeal of the 1910 prohibition on gaming did not have an immediate effect on the city. The card playing and dice rolling that had been going on behind closed doors in the back rooms of saloons and hotels simply moved into the open. There were even those who believed legal gambling would have little impact on the Las Vegas economy.

Journalist William Stymie was one of them. Long before enactment of the new law, he prepared an editorial for the local paper:

> There is much talk and concern among the high brows of the Las Vegas Boosters Club about making games of chance a legal activity in our fair town. I never knew they were illegal. . . . If it is made into a "legal" activity, there will be many more crossroaders and drifters than even the railroad brought in and soon we will need a board of lawyers to keep their eye on the game and a chain gang to keep the civil order. . . . It is the view of this humble reporter that we have enough laws to deal with in Nevada as it is. Gambling . . . a business in Nevada? I doubt it.

Las Vegas moved very cautiously toward its future as a gambling center. It had focused all of its attention on Boulder Dam and many believed that the added inducement of casinos was unnecessary to entertain dam site workers or attract tourists. Open gambling might even invoke the ire of Boulder City boss Sims Ely, a man no one wanted to cross.

Initially, two different authorities were vested with the authority to approve gambling licenses: the Clark County Commission for businesses anywhere in the county and the Las Vegas municipal government for operations within the city limits. The latter decided to limit the number of city gaming licenses to six in April 1931, later revising the figure to ten, but only within the downtown area confined to three blocks on Fremont Street east of Main. This practice of restricting gambling to certain areas of the city gained the name "red lining." Over time, the boundaries would be extended to include the blocks up to Fifth Street, but authorities were careful not to let the red lines overlap residential neighborhoods.

The very first gambling license application to be approved under the new law was submitted by Mayme V. Stocker for the Northern Club at 15 Fremont Street (where the Coin Castle Casino stands, as of this writing). Stocker had arrived in Las Vegas in 1911, a time when gambling was clearly prohibited and the primary forms of public entertainment were swimming, movies, and occasional street corner concerts on Saturday nights. Her husband Oscar worked as an engine foreman for the railroad, and her three sons—Clarence, Harold, and Lester—gradually followed him into railway work as they came of age. The family knew rail workers looked for refreshment at a "Northern Saloon" at every stop, so in 1920, they put together the Las Vegas Northern Club, with Mrs. Stocker designated as the official owner in order to maintain an "arm's length" distance from the railroad business for the Stocker men. The club posed as a soft-drink emporium, but everyone who saw the Northern name knew the proprietress served alcohol. Cleverly, she avoided straight liquor, which could easily be detected by federal agents, and proffered only mixed drinks—harder to prove as violations of Prohibition. The whiskey she used in her beverages was supplied by her son Harold, who owned a share in a local bootleg distillery.

When the gambling law was enacted, Stocker and her Northern Club manager, Joe H. Morgan, knew it was a profitable opportunity to entertain their patrons. Morgan had dealt cards in Tijuana, Mexico after World War I and had seen first-hand how the gambling money could pour in. The license they received was for slot machines, the only kind of permit allowed in the beginning. Their lead was soon followed by neighboring enterprises, including hotels, cafes, and even a sweets shop, as C.J. MacKay obtained a license to install three "one-armed bandits" in his Nevada Hotel Confectionery. The metamorphosis of Fremont Street into Casino Center had begun.

Until 1931, most of the buildings along Fremont were two-story wood and brick structures that housed bakeries, banks, drugstores, and barber shops. The bars, illegal gambling, and prostitution were all centered on Block 16. As the slot machines proliferated, one of the downtown shopkeepers decided to transform his hardware store at 22 Fremont Street into a dedicated gaming hall with a Western motif, including a hitching post for horses out front, sawdust on the floorboards, slot machines lining the walls, and four tables for playing craps, faro, and blackjack. Named the 21 Club, this grand-daddy of Las Vegas casinos operated from mid-1931 until October 1934, when it reopened as the Barrel House, this time sporting a German beer-hall décor with the addition of roulette to its line-up of games. It was the first casino makeover in a city that would ultimately become famous for its never-ending progression of facelifts.

On March 19, 1932, the city's first truly plush hotel-casino would open its doors in the new gaming district, on the northwest corner of Second and Fremont. Designed by noted architect A.L. Worswick and constructed by renowned builder Pietro Orlando Silvagni, the three-story Apache Hotel featured the city's first elevator to provide access to its record-setting 100 rooms and a third-floor banquet hall with a capacity for 300. The Apache Bar and Casino, furnished at a cost of $50,000, set the standard for elegance in southern Nevada. This would become the hub of downtown social life for two decades to come, where local business deals were made and everyone who was anyone sipped a drink, placed a bet, stayed a night, or traded a tale when visiting Las Vegas. The building still stands today behind the enveloping signs of Binion's Horseshoe Hotel and Casino at 128 Fremont.

Whether satisfied with their success in Las Vegas or simply intrigued by green fields elsewhere, the Stocker family, who had kicked off the Fremont Street transformation, decided to move to Moapa Valley in 1932. They left partner Joe Morgan with the Northern Club and he soon proceeded with his wife Helen to open a second, larger gaming spot, the Silver Club on First Street. Working the roulette wheel and dealing the card games, Helen Morgan became the city's first female dealer—or at least the first to deal legally. The Silver Club, with a capacity for 300 players, also touted itself as the first Fremont establishment to install a neon sign, but that claim is disputed by another early entrant into the gambling trade, the Boulder Club, which opened to serve dam site workers in 1929 and 1930. Quite certainly, the Boulder Club gained fame when a blazing electric light display was added to its façade in 1934. The club's signage was created by the Young Electric Sign Company of Ogden, Utah, which would open a full-service sign facility in Las Vegas in the next decade and eventually become responsible for roughly three-quarters of the glowing lights seen in the city by 1985. Who really brought the glow of neon to Fremont may never be settled, but it is certain that casinos up and down the street (notably J. Kell Houssels's Las Vegas Club, the Apache, and the Northern) quickly followed suit, so that by the end of the 1930s, the downtown gambling district was ablaze with colorful lights.

Despite the red-lining by city officials, Fremont Street was not the only place where Las Vegans and dam site workers could part with their money at slots and gaming tables during the 1930s. Even as Mayme Stocker had been getting approval for her license at the Northern Club, another entrepreneur was approaching the Clark County Commission for the first gambling permit outside the Las Vegas city limits, a visionary entrepreneur from California named Tony Cornero.

Also known as "the Admiral," Cornero had been a bootlegger in the 1920s. He was caught landing booze by small craft on the beaches of southern California and spent some time in federal prison before showing up in Las Vegas in 1930 with his brothers Frank and Louis. His aim was to build a nightclub, not within already teeming Block 16, but on the road to the new dam, a first and last stop for workers coming into the city for entertainment. Cornero's idea was to create a place with class—floors covered by carpets instead of sawdust; hot running water and electric lights in every room—where guests could wear their Sunday best instead of dusty boots and jeans.

As a convicted felon, Cornero enlisted his brothers to obtain the necessary permits, including a gambling license from Clark County. They had purchased land at the corner of Fremont and Charleston, where the Boulder Highway begins, and soon started construction on the Meadows, a $31,000 resort-casino with 30 guest rooms, a large gaming area, a dance floor, and its own floor show choreographed by stage-show producer Jack Laughlin. One of the first entertainment acts to appear there in 1931 was the Gumm Sisters, including Frances Gumm, later known to the world as Judy Garland.

If his timing and choice of location had been better, Tony Cornero might have been hailed in years to come as "the man who invented Las Vegas." As luck would have it, the Meadows' success was extremely brief. On Labor Day 1931, the hotel accommodations were gutted when Las Vegas firefighters refused to go outside their jurisdiction to battle a blaze that had started there. Short of cash and unable to promote the high life they envisioned in the midst of the Depression, the Cornero brothers had to sell their interest in the hotel portion of the luxurious resort to southern California hotelier Alex L. Richmond just two months after its grand opening. The Corneros hung on to the casino business until early 1932, but the cash flow for continuing just wasn't there. The brothers split up, with the Admiral heading off to start a floating casino called the S.S. *Rex* off the coast of California. That venture, too, would eventually fail, and Cornero would return to Las Vegas in the 1940s. By then, however, the Meadows would be no more. A Montgomery-Ward store would occupy and then fail on the same land. A new Lowe's Home Center has been erected there now, hopefully without the bad fortune of its predecessors.

Elsewhere near Las Vegas in the 1930s, another club builder had a similar idea— perhaps not as grandiose as Cornero's, but equally grounded in the belief that an entertainment site outside the city limits could capture visitors (and money) before they reached the Fremont Street establishments. Frank Detra and his wife Angelina acquired some land on the Los Angeles Highway, where they opened, owned, and operated the Pair-O-Dice Club in 1931. For the next eight years, the Detras' nightclub would offer Italian meals, music, cocktails, and of course table games, catering to growing crowds of tourists coming up from California to see Boulder Dam. By no means the luxurious stop that Cornero attempted to develop, the Pair-O-Dice Club's table linens were handmade by the owner, lamps with playing-card and dice motifs lit the interior, and perhaps the only adornments bordering on opulence were art deco brass ashtrays and an ornate credenza imported from Germany.

It would be a mistake, however, to overestimate the interest that Las Vegas citizens took in legalized gambling during the 1930s. For all the lights and action that gaming brought, and all the revenue that would one day follow, the city continued to think of itself first and foremost as the "Gateway to Boulder Dam," a tourist stop, not a gambling capital. By 1938, roughly three-quarters of the 200,000-some visitors to the dam stopped in Las Vegas. When fighting broke out in Europe in 1939, Americans' travel abroad was restricted and the city sought to woo vacationers to its many attractions. Besides Boulder Dam, those included Lake Mead, Zion National Park, and the Grand Canyon, all near at hand, as well as (thanks to now-bountiful electric power) the country's highest concentration of air-conditioned rooms, a huge novelty for those used to the swamp coolers of the previous decade.

Cures for a Decade of Depression

In 1940, describing Las Vegas as part of "Tour 3" in a government-sponsored guidebook to the state of Nevada, members of the WPA Writers' Program captured the true spirit of the young city in these words:

> Relatively little emphasis is placed on the gambling clubs and divorce facilities—although they are attractions to many visitors—and much effort is being made to build up cultural attractions. No cheap and easily parodied slogans have been adopted to publicize the city, no attempt has been made to introduce pseudo-romantic architectural themes, or to give artificial glamor and gaiety. Las Vegas is itself—natural and therefore very appealing to people with a wide variety of interests.
>
> All the world meets on the broad sunny streets—eastern businessmen interested in studying the amazing powerhouse 20 miles away on the river, and in playing a bit of roulette in the evenings, health-seekers basking in the brilliant sunshine, an occasional Paiute woman with a baby cradled on her back, toothless prospectors in town for a grubstake, cowboys rolling along in elaborate high-heeled boots, ranchers and their wives buying supplies and seeing movies, young people rushing down to Lake Mead to swim or up to camp or ski in the Charleston Mountains, men and women of any age on their way to the stables for horses, local men and women going to rehearsals of the little theater group.

If Nevada had a flashy gambling capital in the 1930s, it was Reno, not Las Vegas. Before games of chance could become central to the Las Vegas economy, two more elements were required, neither of which any city planner could have anticipated—the advent of war and the arrival of organized crime.

Chapter Four

FROM AIR STRIP TO "THE" STRIP

Just like the 1930s, with its chain of political and economic events that helped save Las Vegas from becoming just another ghost town, the 1940s brought World War II and a helping hand for the struggling city from the United States government. President Franklin Roosevelt had announced the need to strengthen western air defenses and the strategic location of Old Fort Baker was once again a focus of attention.

In June 1940, the War Department launched the first segment of its militarization of Las Vegas by constructing a small auxiliary base to park, fuel, and service navy planes at Boulder City's airport. But a bigger location was needed to enact the government's plans for Army Air Corps operations in the valley. An airfield owned by Western Air Express, 8 miles northeast of Las Vegas, was being considered for take-over, but it would require cooperation between the city, state, and federal authorities, as well as the agreement of the private company that owned the land. In previous years, Western Air had balked at all offers to purchase the field.

Instrumental in cobbling the eventual deal was former Las Vegas postmaster Robert Griffith, whose father Edward W. had opened the Majestic Theatre in 1912. Bob Griffith was an aviation expert who had some pull with Nevada's Senator Pat McCarran. Together, they successfully lobbied for the federal funds needed to make the plan come together. With political influence and cash in hand, in October 1940 the City of Las Vegas was able to purchase the property and then immediately offered to lease it to the Army Air Corps for $1 a year. Local officials believed the new facilities would be used for joint military and commercial endeavors—in effect, a new airport for the city—supported by $340,000 pledged for upgrades by the Civil Aeronautics Authority.

The rental deal became official on January 23, 1941, but it turned out that the War Department had other plans for the location. Instead of an airbase, it was to become an air training school—the hub of an expansive shooting range where army pilots and gunners could prepare for airborne combat. Intense building efforts got quickly underway to add hangars, barracks, storage areas, fuel depots, and three runways at a cost of $25 million. Under court order, federal marshals cleared all residents from 1 million acres of sparsely populated land in Clark and Nye Counties to be used as a restricted training zone. Within nine months, all preparations were completed. The leased field and gunnery range would eventually be touted as "the largest tactical air facility in the Free World."

Throughout the war, the Las Vegas Air Gunnery School (later named the Las Vegas Army Air Field) taught soldiers to man machine guns on the B-17 Flying Fortresses and later the B-29 Super Fortress. The entire wartime history of the base was one of innovation in equipment and teaching techniques, which were later duplicated at other locations throughout the country. By 1942, the gunnery school was graduating students at a rate of 4,000 every six weeks. In 1944, the training range was expanded to 3.3 million acres. By the spring of 1945, the bombers based at Las Vegas and nearby Indian Springs were joined by fighter planes, increasing the facility's total manpower to nearly 13,000 men and women.

Not only did this amazing metamorphous of military might and personnel increase the United States' security, power, and morale, but on the practical side, it also brought a welcome increase to the number of visitors on Fremont Street. The gunnery school personnel and the Las Vegas citizenry quickly became friendly and cooperative with each other. While the new barracks were being built, many residents opened their homes to the servicemen. Throughout the war, several of the local casinos presented their own floorshows free of charge at the base theatres. And of course, more than a little of the military payroll found its way into Las Vegas gaming halls and saloons, and the pockets of local business owners.

One place War Department funds did not end up, however, was in the brothels of Block 16. Up until the early 1940s, prostitution was still legal in Las Vegas, if only confined by ordinance to the recognized red light district. Fearful of "offending the morals of young America," the military forced the governing authorities in 1942 to put an end to legal prostitution, not only in Las Vegas, but throughout all of Clark County. Local ladies of the night took the shut-down surprisingly well. They simply took their business to other areas of southern Nevada—such as nearby Nye and Esmeralda Counties—where "the oldest profession in the world" was (and is) still legal.

In 1946, a handful of bordello proponents would try to revive the age-old practice, not in Block 16, but at the Formyle Club on Boulder Highway and the Kassabian Ranch just south of the Las Vegas city limits. Their moves raised the ire of Mormons, Catholics, and Protestants alike, as well as the Las Vegas Chamber of Commerce, which had long sought to promote a positive and wholesome image for the community. The Las Vegas Hospital Association provided data showing how the end of prostitution had brought about a decline in venereal disease in the city. School Superintendent Maude Frazier added that sexually transmitted diseases had been a problem at Las Vegas High School prior to the 1942 closing of the brothels, but not in evidence at all thereafter. Backed by such public outcries, county officials empowered Sheriff Glen Jones to enforce the law, revoking business licenses and closing down the offenders. The commissioners later drafted even stronger statutes to see that prostitution would never return. Till this very day, sex-for-money services have remained technically illegal in Clark County and a vice forever banned in the city that is ironically often cited as synonymous with sin.

After the war was over, the military training facility suspended operations, but the gunnery school partially reopened in 1947, then expanded through 1949 to ready itself for a new mission: preparing jet fighter pilots for combat in Korea. In May 1950, the base, with a mixed fleet of prop and jet planes, was officially renamed Nellis Air Force Base, honoring First Lieutenant William Harrell Nellis, a southern Nevada airman whose P-47 Thunderbolt was shot down over Luxembourg on December 27, 1944 as he attempted his 70th mission. In the decades to follow, Nellis AFB would play an important role in every major maneuver undertaken by the military, from napalm-bomb training for missions in Indochina in the 1960s and 1970s to readying "top guns" for Operation Desert Storm in the Middle East in the 1990s. The base would be instrumental in testing new weapons and aircraft such as the U-2 spy plane, the Blackhawk helicopter, and the Stealth bomber. It would also become the permanent home of the United States Air Force Air Demonstration Squadron—the elite precision-flying team better known as the Thunderbirds.

So the city never got its desired airport on the old Western Air Express site. The intended commercial section there, which had originally been dedicated McCarran Field, was deeded over to the government in 1948. But thanks to a bond issue approved by Clark County voters in May 1947, there were sufficient funds to purchase a small private landing strip on Highway 91, south of Las Vegas. It was originally called Alamo Airfield, so-named in 1942 by owner George Crockett, who happened to be a descendant of frontiersman Davy Crockett. From 1948, it became known as Clark County Public Airport, then the new McCarran Field, and it would handle 16 passenger flights a day by 1950.

As the conflict in Europe and the Pacific came to an end, American citizens' thoughts turned readily to travel and leisure. Not surprisingly, Nevada was high on the list of veterans and young honeymooners alike, although their destination was still more likely to be the state's better-developed resort, Reno, than Las Vegas. In the mid-1940s, the gaming center to the north outstripped its southern rival by a ratio of 5 to 2 in terms of population and even greater in tourism revenue.

Recognizing there was an opportunity to capture some of Reno's wealth, Edmund Converse organized Bonanza Air Lines in 1945 to provide commercial flights between Las Vegas and "the world's biggest little city." United Airlines would follow his lead with air links of its own two years later. TWA and Western drew Las Vegas into their route maps as well. Converse's venture would not only succeed in gaining tourist dollars for Las Vegas, but it would also prove to be a lucrative investment for its founder when purchased in 1968 by another airline visionary, Howard Hughes, to become Hughes Air West. Air travel would ever after play a major role in the city's ability to attract visitors.

Besides trained pilots and soldiers, America's successful war effort also required basic minerals, such as iron, copper, and tin. One particularly essential element was magnesium, a plentiful supply of which was discovered buried in the foothills 15 miles southeast of Las Vegas. Under the direction of the national government's Defense Plants Corporation, Basic Magnesium, Inc. (BMI) was established in 1942 to mine and refine the land's rich veins of ore for the production of aircraft parts, engines, and incendiary bombs. The new plant required workers by the thousands and, before long, it became the nation's biggest supplier of the much-needed mineral.

Owing to the war-induced manpower shortage, women took up many of the jobs that heretofore would have been considered man's work. They drove forklifts, operated lathes, poured molten metal, stacked ingots, and otherwise carried out every function expected of men at the BMI plant. Wearing gas masks and asbestos gloves to protect themselves from toxic fumes and burns, they braved daytime indoor temperatures of 130 degrees Fahrenheit and worked shifts of up to 12 hours straight for standard pay of 90¢ an hour, the same amount their male counterparts earned. When demand for magnesium slowed toward the end of the war, the factory and its workers would shift to production of munitions for Rheem Manufacturing Company.

Around the BMI mining operation, a new community sprang up—Henderson, Nevada—which was named after the former Nevada senator who served on Basic Magnesium's board of directors, Charles Belnap Henderson. The new plant and town brought employment, population growth, and cash flow to the Las Vegas Valley, but they also fueled a growing fire of discord—racial discrimination.

As of 1940, only 5.6 percent of the entire Nevada population was considered non-white. The vast majority of those were Native Americans, who resided mainly on their reservations. The census listed only 664 African Americans statewide. The equal-opportunity employment offered by the Army Air Corps facility and Basic Magnesium attracted workers of all colors. Nevada's African-American population would grow almost sevenfold in the 1940s as a result.

White Las Vegans, many of whom had migrated from the deep south, were not at all happy with this influx of African Americans. The limited tolerance they had shown for African Americans in the 1930s turned to hate and Jim Crow prohibitions, then outright attempts to force the "unwelcome race" out of town. One such attempt was the creation of the Carver Park Housing Project in Henderson in 1943. Ostensibly under the management of African Americans like Lubertha Johnson, the project was supposed to house Basic Magnesium's black workers and keep them segregated from the whites. But the workers never bought into it. Although modern, Carver Park was in an isolated area. Preferring to live among the African-American community in Las Vegas, the workers refused to move in and the housing project eventually had to be abandoned unoccupied.

Johnson herself quit the project and bought a ranch in Paradise Valley between Henderson and Las Vegas, where she would host annual picnics for the local chapter of the NAACP. In 1945, she began working for the Las Vegas Housing Authority to open the city's first public housing project on the west side of town, an area which is even today considered a predominantly non-white neighborhood.

In fact, the exodus of African-American residents and business owners "across the tracks" from the city's downtown area to West Las Vegas was a singular phenomenon of the 1940s. Some said they wanted to avoid tax increases and take advantage of lower land costs on the Westside. Others insist that the police chief and Mayor Ernie Cragin had threatened to revoke or not renew their business licenses if they didn't vacate the city center. In any event, the disappearance of "colored" faces on Fremont Street was noticeable and obvious, just as were the separate toilet facilities for whites and non-whites at the Basic Magnesium plant site. Such incidents of segregation and racial discrimination proliferated for more than a decade, not only in the valley but throughout the state, earning Nevada the dubious title "Mississippi of the West."

As conditions between whites and blacks worsened, for the area's residents of Japanese descent, they hit rock bottom. The *issei* (first-generation Japanese Americans), who came to the valley as farmers after 1913, had met with considerable difficulty in farming and in attempts to integrate themselves within the Las Vegas economy. In 1920, the *issei* and their family members numbered 62 in Clark County. Twenty years later, their numbers had fallen to 49. Most of them kept a low profile in the community, partly due to language and cultural differences, but also because of anti-Japanese sentiments that reached a crescendo with the bombing of Pearl Harbor by Japanese aircraft in December 1941.

Yonema "Bill" Tomiyasu was among the few successful *issei* in the valley. He had moved to Las Vegas in 1916, married the following year, and started out by growing alfalfa. In the years that followed, he raised crops of onions, carrots, cabbages, asparagus, beets, and a wide variety of other vegetables and fruit—even melons (particularly difficult to cultivate in the arid environs), which earned unsolicited praise from the *Las Vegas Review-Journal*. Tomiyasu's produce became a staple of many local restaurants. And when construction began on Boulder Dam in the 1930s, the high quality of his vegetables won him a long-term contract with the Six Companies of the Boulder Dam project to supply their construction camp mess halls with food.

On March 18, 1942, President Roosevelt signed Executive Order No. 9102, which established the War Relocation Authority. Operating within the Office for Emergency Management, the new civilian agency was charged with "removing certain persons or classes of people from designated areas," notably anyone of Japanese race living near the Pacific Coast. Ten relocation camps were quickly created, including several in California and Arizona, with a capacity to house more than 110,000 Japanese Americans. Soon Japanese Nevadans found themselves under surveillance and the FBI dispatched agents to restrict their movement, especially in the vicinity of Boulder Dam, which was considered a potential military target.

From Air Strip to "The" Strip

Thanks to the high respect Clark County citizens had for Tomiyasu's horticultural talent, he and his family were spared the painful shame of internment. In fact, only one southern Nevada issei is known to have been sent to the camps, an avowed enemy sympathizer whose political views attracted the attention of federal authorities. To prove his own loyalty and support for his adopted home, Tomiyasu arranged the delivery of poultry, fruit, and vegetables to the Las Vegas Air Gunnery School during the war years. He brought his children home from California colleges to work on the farm and he hired an issei friend from San Bernardino as a laborer in order to release him from internment in Poston, Arizona. Following state policy, Tomiyasu dutifully surrendered any items deemed contraband, such as cameras, flashlights, and radio parts. Not embittered by the experience, the veteran farmer accepted this difficult period as fate. After the war, he would turn his attention from growing crops to raising shrubbery, developing a nursery business that he ran profitably until the 1960s.

By contrast, a very different group of "foreigners" was being welcomed to southern Nevada in the 1940s—Mexicans. In fact, it is only since World War II that large numbers of Hispanics have moved to the Las Vegas Valley. After gambling was legalized in 1931, aliens had been banned by the Nevada legislature from operating gaming houses or gambling devices in Clark County. In practice, that meant anyone who resembled a non-white (Mexican Americans in particular) was denied employment in the burgeoning casinos. Discrimination had similarly kept Hispanics from union jobs and some of the best positions working for the railway. But with the shortage of labor caused by the war, demand could not be met for miners, construction and farm workers, railroad hands, busboys, dishwashers, maids, and janitors. At least temporarily, anti-Hispanic employment practices had to be put aside.

In 1942, the United States and Mexican governments signed an agreement whereby workers could come north of the border to fill vacancies, especially on farms and for the rail companies. The Union Pacific was among the first to embrace this so-called "Bracero Program." Farms around Las Vegas and Moapa Valleys also benefited. What were only a handful of Hispanics in the Las Vegas–area population grew to 3,174 by the close of the decade. Of those, seven out of ten lived in the city proper. This migration helped fuel the segregation trends mentioned earlier, however, and those newcomers who did not settle on outlying farms ended up, by and large, in the depressed areas of the Westside or North Las Vegas.

What improvements were being made to the city's infrastructure during the war years were centered on the business district and residential areas east of Main Street. For example, a new railroad depot was built to replace the southwestern-style terminal; this one featured spiffy, Art Deco "moderne" architecture. One section of town in particular experienced a renaissance: the Huntridge Addition. This neighborhood occupies a 140-acre area southeast of the original Clark Townsite, between Charleston and Oakey Boulevards. Maryland Parkway, with its separated lanes looping north and south around oval-shaped Huntridge Circle Park, is its centerpiece. Street names there read like a who's who of 1940s Las Vegas: Bracken and Griffith; (Cyril S.) Wengert, after the city's prominent businessman-banker; and (George) Franklin for the chairman of the Clark County Commission. Its homes were typical of the day, with spacious front yards and plenty of greenery, from tropical palms and desert mesquite to stately firs and broad-leafed shade trees—even lush lawns of grass.

Residents who grew up in the neighborhood say it was an idyllic place to be raised. In those days, there was no reason for door locks or bars on the windows. A few local businesses still retain the Huntridge name, such as a drugstore and a popular old bar. Many of the original 500 houses built there during the war period still stand, retaining their pleasant mid-century appeal and owned by some of the community's longest residents. Perhaps the neighborhood's most famous celebrity, however, is not a person at all; the Huntridge Theatre, built in 1944 and designed by Beverly Hills architect A.B. Heinsbergen, became a popular movie house for years. It was where children enjoyed matinees on Saturday afternoons. The house was always jam-packed when the latest Disney movies appeared there. Its Art Deco tower, located on the southeastern corner of Charleston and Maryland Parkway, has always been the district's most-recognizable landmark. As a publicity stunt, Frank Sinatra once sold tickets at the Huntridge for his movie Suddenly, which made its debut there. Other stars, such as Bud Abbott and Lou Costello, Marlene Dietrich, and Vincent Price, also made personal appearances at the theater. In 1999, the Huntridge was added to the National Registry of Historical Places and thanks to the terms of current ownership, its presence is protected until at least 2017.

The population of 13,937 that greater Las Vegas counted in 1940 grew by leaps and bounds during the war years, reaching nearly 35,000 by 1942. Housing shortages forced the opening of other residential areas—the Mayfair Tract, the Baltimore Addition, and Kelso-Turner Terrace—and some 1,166 new dwellings were added in all. Only reluctantly did the Las Vegas Land and Water Company agree to provide water to the new units. The number of private wells therefore increased from 275 to 450 in the nine years following 1935, once more lowering the water table and threatening the city's supply. In fact, in 1944, the Nevada state engineer told the local chamber of commerce that Las Vegas was again running out of water.

Many believed that the return to a peacetime economy would cause an inevitable exodus of the military and its civilian workforce, but that was not the case. By the end of the 1940s, the area's populace swelled to 45,577, roughly half of them crowded within the city limits proper. Local officials again considered drastic action. In a 1948 referendum, voters approved the creation of the Las Vegas Valley Water District and charged it with two important goals: to buy out the existing water company—which had controlled the area's springs, wells, storage, and distribution system since 1905—and to bring the waters gathered behind Hoover Dam to Las Vegas. The latter would be accomplished by using the facilities of BMI, which had languished since the war.

Unfortunately, the plan to tap Lake Mead's reservoir could not be implemented quickly enough. During the summer of 1949, faucets began to run dry, including those on the second floor of Las Vegas Hospital. Per capita consumption of water gradually rose to 800 gallons a day, an estimated 80 percent of it spread on lawns or otherwise wasted. As a countermeasure, Mayor Ernie Cragin invoked a ban on lawn sprinkling between the hours of 9 a.m. and 5 p.m. This action would be followed by the city's first increase in water rates in two decades, to a basic charge of $2.70 per month. But real relief for the parched community would not arrive until 1955, when the quenching resources of Lake Mead at last reached the water district's distribution system.

Why had the city continued to grow so actively after the war? In a word, the answer was "tourism." But the sunny story of Las Vegas' transformation into America's tourist Mecca has its dark side. In California, lawmakers had moved since the late 1930s to rid their state of criminal elements, illegal gambling hall operators in particular. Feeling the heat, many of these renegade entrepreneurs turned their attention and money to Nevada, where gambling had been made legal since 1931. Among them was the alleged boss of underground gaming in Los Angeles—Captain Guy McAfee.

McAfee was a Los Angeles vice squad commander who secretly owned illegal casinos. In 1939, he saw opportunity gleaming just south of Las Vegas on a dusty 7-mile portion of Highway 91 used by travelers going from southern California to Utah. He purchased the original Pair-O-Dice Club from the Detra family, renovated the nightclub property to focus on gambling, and reopened it as the 91 Club, just in time to coincide with Clark Gable's highly publicized Las Vegas divorce from Ria Langham. As a joke, he often compared the lonely stretch of highway running past his club to Los Angeles's busy Sunset Strip. Prophetically, the optimistic tag stuck and the desolate thoroughfare—much later named Las Vegas Boulevard—has been known as "The Strip" ever since.

The early success of the 91 Club emboldened McAfee to move uptown. As wartime military personnel poured into the area, he expanded his casino ownership to Fremont Street, purchasing in 1942 what was then considered the "best-run gambling enterprise in Las Vegas," the Pioneer Club, from four gamblers who had similarly been forced to leave California—Bill Curland, Chuck Addision, Farmer Paige, and Tudor Scherer. By 1945, this downtown investment enabled the former police officer to open yet another small casino, the Frontier Club at the corner of First Street. An openly enthusiastic promoter of gambling, McAfee brought in Hollywood friends to visit his clubs, including movie stars William Powell and Cary Grant. Excellent management and marketing techniques, backed by plentiful California capital, allowed the captain to parlay one good investment into another, making him—for a while, at least—the kingpin of Las Vegas gambling.

That is not to say he had no rivals. In 1941, still another displaced Californian, John Grayson, established the El Cortez Hotel and Casino on the northeast corner of Fremont and Sixth, extending the range of city center commercial properties farther to the east, where suburban homes were relocated or razed. His original partners were Las Vegas Club owner J. Kell Houssels and real estate developer Marion Hicks, who would play a key role in Las Vegas casino expansion through the next decade. Meanwhile, Tony Cornero had returned to Las Vegas in 1944 and leased the Apache Hotel's casino operations, which he renamed the S.S. Rex Club, after his failed California cruise line venture.

A much bigger threat to McAfee's domination of local gambling, however, was looming to the south. Even as the captain was staking his claims on Fremont Street, another Californian was getting ready to challenge his ownership of the Strip with something more ambitious than a simple gaming club. Thomas Hull, the successful owner of three identically-named El Rancho properties in California, had the revolutionary idea of building a similar kind of resort in the "boondocks" of Las Vegas. Two local businessmen, Bob Griffith and car dealer James "Big Jim" Cashman, had convinced the hotelier that the best site would be outside the city limits, where taxes were lower, water rights were not questioned, and land was cheap. Hull confidently purchased 133 acres on the southwest corner of Highway 91 and San Francisco Street (now Sahara Avenue) for just $150 per acre.

The woman who sold the land to Hull was astonished, as she had considered the acreage "worthless." Hull, on the other hand, saw vast possibilities in providing a cool and convenient rest stop for weary travelers, offering the added enticement of gambling, which was now legal throughout Clark County, except in Boulder City. He designed this property with the same theme as the others, in a Spanish Mission style, with a distinctive windmill atop the main building. At night, the windmill was lit in neon, a beacon for travelers. By day, the resort was also a welcoming sight, with its grassy lawns, inviting swimming pool, and ranch-style motel rooms encircling the main restaurant and casino. Hull also added some shops and offered horseback riding to his guests, as well as other amenities.

The famous El Rancho sign was designed by the same Young Electric Sign Company (YESCO) which set downtown Las Vegas aglow in the 1930s. YESCO founder Thomas Young was born in 1895 in England, but soon moved to Ogden, Utah with his parents and siblings. The family had adopted the Mormon faith shortly before making their journey to the "promised land." With an excellent work ethic, Young opened his first sign shop in Ogden in 1920 and became famous locally for the excellent craftsmanship of his work. In 1932, shortly after gambling had been reinstated in Nevada, Young's company began serving Las Vegas by building the important signs outside the clubs on Fremont Street. In 1945, Young established a branch office in Las Vegas and the city's first spectacular neon sign was created for the Boulder Club. Soon after, all the casinos on

Fremont Street wanted signs like the Boulder Club and the race was on, adding "neon" to gold, silver, and water as the most precious commodities in Las Vegas. As the Strip grew, so did its colorful signage and the unmistakable signature of YESCO.

The El Rancho had its grand opening on April 3, 1941 and was a success from the very beginning. Its original 40 cottages soon expanded to 220 rooms. The gambling area was small by today's standards, featuring only one craps table, two blackjack tables, and a roulette wheel, but it served as the model for future casinos. Within a year, it gained notoriety as the place where Clark Gable stayed and paced the floor, after learning that a plane carrying his wife, Carole Lombard, had crashed on January 16, 1942. Gable flew immediately to Las Vegas from Lockheed Airport via chartered plane. A search party was sent out, but only the most experienced climbers were able to get to the crash scene. Once there, they learned the terrible truth: no one had survived.

Newspapers across the country made headline news of the tragedy. Lombard had traveled by train from Los Angeles to a war bond rally in Indianapolis, where she helped raise $2.5 million for the war effort. Flying back to Hollywood with her mother and agent, the starlet had landed in Las Vegas to await refueling. Her onward flight went down in the Potosi Mountain Range on Table Mountain (also referred to as Double or Nothing Peak in news accounts at the time). Although the night had been clear and the pilot experienced, for some reason the flight strayed 6 miles off course. Had the pilot veered just a few yards, the peak could have been avoided. What caused the crash would never be known.

Until 1960, the El Rancho prospered through various owners and several expansions, always offering the best in name entertainment (Milton Berle, Jackie Gleason, Dean Martin and Jerry Lewis, and Peggy Lee, among others) and what would become a Las Vegas staple: scantily-clad showgirls. The latter included the George Moro dancers, choreographed with the assistance of Ruth Landis in the 1940s, and Minneapolis-born stripper Lili St. Cyr, who gained fame in the 1950s by taking bubble baths on the El Rancho stage. The Minnesota temptress frequently shared the bill with popular comedian Joe E. Lewis and they made quite a successful team. Authors Best and Hilyer described St. Cyr as follows:

> a stripper deluxe who appears on stage in such radiant undress that audiences are rendered not only speechless but gaspless. Her appeal is particularly demonstrated by the finale of an act called "Bird in a Gilded Cage," in which she soars out over the audience in a gilded cage, dropping beaded panties, frilly garters, and sequined bras on the hands-outstretched spectators below.

Shrewd businessman that he was, McAfee decided not to compete with Hull on the dusty Strip. He discovered that a certain Texas businessman, who owned a chain of 475 movie theaters across the Southwest, was looking for properties he could develop into a string of hotels. What's more, cinema-magnate R.E. Griffith (no relation to E.W. or Bob Griffith) saw the land south of El Rancho as an ideal site for a competing resort-casino. Only one item disturbed the appeal of the lot—it was currently the location of Guy McAfee's 91 Club. If Griffith wanted to build, he would simply have to buy the club out. Negotiating between the two men was reportedly intense. The price of land in the area had naturally gone up with the success of the El Rancho. After considerable dickering, a price of $1,000 an acre was agreed on for the 35-acre property. Afterwards, it was said that McAfee told Griffith, "If you'd bargained harder, I would've sold for less." Griffith allegedly replied, "If you'd bargained harder, I would've paid more."

The new land owner quickly assigned his nephew, architect William J. Moore, to design his envisioned motel-casino resort, the Last Frontier. Moore later said that the object was to make it as authentically Western as they could. They even brought in talented Navajo Indians to set stone that had been quarried in nearby Red Rock Canyon. The ceilings were high, set with cross beams, featuring a huge fireplace in the center. The hotel's Gay Nineties Bar was transported and reassembled from the old Arizona Club in the Las Vegas red-light district. The bar itself was a beautiful, antiqued mahogany gem, with bar stools designed to look like western saddles. An especially noteworthy design innovation was the El Rancho's swimming pool, which was placed in front of the low-rise hotel instead of the customary location in the rear.

Griffith and Moore met with some problems along the way that Hull's El Rancho Vegas managed to avoid, due to timing. Specifically, World War II had begun and materials were in short supply. The Army Air Corps rapidly confiscated building supplies for the war effort "under government authority" just as quickly as the hotel makers acquired them. However, Moore managed to come up with construction materials from a secret source—deserted mines. The young architect arranged to purchase two abandoned mine sites in Pioche, then dispatched crews of men to strip them of wiring and conduits, casings, pipes, control switches, and every other useful item they could carry away. Had the War Production Board discovered Moore's actions, the salvaged supplies would surely have been confiscated.

The grand opening of the Last Frontier took place on October 30, 1942 and it proved to be another huge success. The front-facing pool could be easily seen from the highway, serving as a kind of mirage to attract weary and dusty travelers. Moore then went one step further and added a Western Frontier Village to the north end of the property, including a wedding chapel called the Little Church of the West. The church was a quaint structure, modeled after an Old West mining town chapel. Its interior was redwood, the outside cedar. Its romantic and nostalgic atmosphere attracted many celebrities who tied the knot there, including the first couple, Betty Grable and Harry James, in 1943. The building itself would be moved

Before the Old Spanish Trail brought settlers to the region in the mid-nineteenth century, nomadic Southern Paiute Indians claimed the Las Vegas Valley as their home. (Courtesy UNLV Special Collections.)

"America's Moses," Brigham Young (1801– 1877) recognized the strategic importance of Las Vegas and sent his Mormon missionaries to establish a fort here in 1855. (Courtesy LDS Church Archives.)

The flowing waters of Las Vegas Creek made "the meadows" a desert oasis for ranching and homesteading following the Civil War. (Courtesy UNLV Special Collections.)

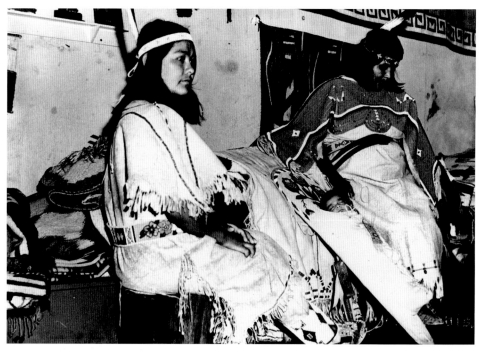

As Las Vegas was striving to become a city, the Southern Nevada Paiutes struggled to retain their tribal culture and home. (Courtesy Nevada State Library and Archives.)

The powerful senator from Montana, William A. Clark (1839–1925), waving, brought the railroad to Las Vegas. His land auction marked the official beginning of the town on May 15, 1905. (Courtesy UNLV Special Collections.)

Until a permanent rail depot could be built at the Las Vegas water stop, this converted rail car served the purpose for the San Pedro, Los Angeles and Salt Lake Railway, c. 1905. (Courtesy UNLV Special Collections.)

The very first "First Lady of Las Vegas" was Helen Stewart (1854–1926), whose fortitude and compassion gained her respect throughout the Valley. She took special interest in the local Paiutes and their basket craft, deeding land to the tribe in 1911 as a permanent home. (Courtesy UNLV Special Collections.)

Peter Buol (1873–1939) was the first mayor of Las Vegas, elected to office on June 1, 1911, when the Las Vegas city charter was approved. (Courtesy UNLV Special Collections.)

Las Vegas' reputation as an "anything goes" frontier town was based mainly on the bars and bordellos of Block 16, one of only two sections of the city zoned to serve up alcohol and sex. (Courtesy UNLV Special Collections

The Arizona Club was the hub of social activity in Block 16. (Courtesy UNLV Special Collections.)

Rail boss Walter Bracken (1870–1950)—with wife Ann, c. 1910—controlled the city's water rights during its early years. (Courtesy UNLV Special Collections.)

Ladd's Plunge provided an ideal way to beat the summer heat in the 1920s. (Courtesy UNLV Special Collections.)

Snow fell heavily on January 10, 1930, providing a bit of distraction from the concerns of economic depression. (Courtesy UNLV Special Collections.)

Las Vegas was still very much a frontier town in the 1930s. Its "Wild West" image was exemplified by the annual Helldorado celebration begun in 1935. (Courtesy UNLV Special Collections.)

Las Vegas School Superintendent Maude Frazier (1881–1963) was one prominent Clark County citizen of the 1930s. (Courtesy UNLV Special Collections.)

Mayme Stocker (1875–1972), wearing glasses, obtained the city's first gaming license for the Northern Club in 1931. (Courtesy UNLV Special Collections.)

Construction of the new dam created thousands of jobs in the early 1930s, not only for construction workers and engineers but for office staff as well. (Courtesy UNLV Special Collections.)

In 1929, Elks Club members, led by Charles Aplin, erected an arch over Fremont Street, proclaiming the city's gateway status. (Courtesy UNLV Special Collections.)

New Deal construction brought lasting change to the look of Las Vegas. Among buildings still remaining from the Depression Era are the Green Shack Restaurant, built in 1930, and the Post Office and Federal Building, opened in 1933. (Courtesy EZway Books, LLC.)

In October 1943, the Williams family became the first residents of the Carver District in Henderson. (Courtesy UNLV Special Collections.)

Above and opposite page, bottom: The Las Vegas Air Gunnery School trained pilots and gunners for World War II combat at a rate of 4,000 graduates every six weeks. The military changed its name several times, emerging as Nellis Air Force Base in 1950. (Courtesy U.S. Air Force and UNLV Special Collections.)

The Boulder Club was the first downtown casino to install electric signage. (Courtesy YESCO.)

The city's first stand-alone library was opened in 1952. (Courtesy Las Vegas Library.)

The Golden Nugget Gambling Hall opened across the street from the Apache Hotel, defining the downtown corridor that would be known as "Glitter Gulch." (Courtesy UNLV Special Collections.)

Slot machines and table games, such as the "Wheel of Fortune," were outlawed in Nevada from 1910 until 1931, but even after legalization, Las Vegas only slowly embraced gambling as a new revenue source. (Courtesy UNLV Special Collections.)

Finished at a cost of over $6 million, the Flamingo was the first hotel in the world constructed after World War II. Benjamin "Bugsy" Siegel (1905–1947) was murdered shortly after its launch. (Courtesy Vintage Vegas.)

The Las Vegas Chamber of Commerce introduced "Vegas Vic" as a new symbol of the city's friendly frontier hospitality in 1947. This 75-foot high neon welcome sign standing by the Pioneer Club was constructed by Young Electric Sign Company in 1951. The heavyweight mascot tipped the scales at 12,000 pounds. (Courtesy YESCO.)

Despite efforts by the federal government to keep organized crime out of casinos, the Syndicate tightened its grip on Las Vegas gambling in the 1950s, backed in part by pension fund money from the Teamsters Union. (Courtesy Library of Congress.)

The Last Frontier began its incarnation in 1942. It became the New Frontier in 1955, was razed in 1965, reopened as the Frontier in 1967, then reverted to the name it now bears, the New Frontier, in 1998. (Courtesy Vintage Vegas.)

The 1969 comeback of Elvis Presley (1935–1977) at the International Hotel (now the Las Vegas Hilton) marked a resurgence of Las Vegas as the world's entertainment capital. (Courtesy The Hollywood Store.)

On stage at Caesars Palace in 1971, "Mr. Showmanship" was Walter Liberace (1919–1987), whose "glorious excess" made him synonymous with Las Vegas–style entertainment in the 1970s and 1980s. (Courtesy Las Vegas Press Club.)

The Las Vegas Chamber of Commerce chose "Legends in Concert" as the 1985 "Show of the Year." It is still going strong at the Imperial Palace—the longest running production show in Las Vegas history. (Courtesy Las Vegas Press Club.)

Cuban bandmaster Desi Arnaz was one of many Hispanic entertainers popular in Las Vegas in the 1950s. (Courtesy The Hollywood Store.)

The Sahara was one of many projects contracted to Arizona builder Del Webb. His company would later own the property, and Webb became actively involved in local civic affairs, such as the Clark County Boys' Club. (Courtesy Del Webb Corporation.)

The Landmark was the last resort bought by Howard Hughes, not because he was out of money, but because the federal government feared he was creating a gambling monopoly. (Courtesy Vintage Vegas.)

With the creation of Binion's Horseshoe in 1951, Texan Benny Binion (1904–1989) challenged the mob's dominance of local gambling. (Courtesy Binion's Horseshoe.)

The Rat Pack c. 1960 (left to right): Peter Lawford, Sammy Davis Jr., Frank Sinatra, Joey Bishop, and Dean Martin. (Courtesy Comic Two Talent.)

Caesars Palace (above) built a million-dollar arena to host Muhammad Ali's 1980 attempt to win his fourth heavyweight boxing title (opposite page). (Courtesy Patrick Sun and Title Boxing.)

Billionaire Howard Hughes lived in Las Vegas only four years after his arrival in 1966, but he effected more change here than any single man since William Clark founded the town in 1905, paving the way for corporate ownership of casinos. (Courtesy Las Vegas Review Journal.)

Dr. Martin Luther King Jr. (1929–1968), left, met with Las Vegas Mayor Oran Gragson (1911–2002) to discuss civil rights issues and address racial unrest, which plagued the city in the 1960s. The important contributions of both men are honored still in the association of their names with two of the area's roadways. (Courtesy Las Vegas Review-Journal.)

Among professional sports brought to Las Vegas, one of the most popular and enduring is the National Finals Rodeo held each December since 1985. (Courtesy Professional Rodeo Cowboys Association.)

The Las Vegas skyline is as distinctive as the visionaries who created it. (Courtesy Las Vegas News Bureau.)

Magicians Siegfried and Roy began headlining at the Mirage upon its opening in 1989. They have been a Las Vegas attraction ever since. (Courtesy Siegfried and Roy.)

A canopy of lights now covers the downtown Casino Center, as the Fremont Street Experience opened in 1995. (Courtesy Las Vegas News Bureau.)

"Viva Las Vegas" in the twenty-first century: It's about showgirls, showguys, and "show me the money," but a 2002 issue of Money magazine has also shown Las Vegas as the No. 1 place to live in America. (Courtesy Las Vegas News Bureau.)

The Strip turned "family friendly" in the 1990s, as evidenced by the appearance of the World of Coca-Cola, GameWorks, and M&M's World at the Showcase center on South Las Vegas Boulevard. (Courtesy Patrick Sun.)

The desert railroad town that was founded in 1905 bears little resemblance to the Entertainment Capital of the World that Las Vegas has become over the past ten decades. (Courtesy James MacPherson.)

The Stratosphere is not only a Las Vegas landmark; it is an heir to local heritage. Its creator, Bob Stupak, went from "rags to riches"—just like the first casino operators of the 1930s. Months after opening in 1996, plagued by financial problems, the Stratosphere came under new ownership—reminiscent of the original Flamingo that launched the Strip's dreamscapes in the 1940s. Its new owner is a billionaire financier who once ran Trans World Airlines—not unlike Howard Hughes in the 1960s. (Courtesy EZway Books, LLC.)

The future of rapid transit: Scheduled to begin service in 2004, the $650 million Las Vegas Monorail will run from the MGM Grand to the Sahara. (Courtesy Las Vegas Monorail.)

Las Vegas welcomes nearly three million visitors and more than 4,000 new residents each month. (Courtesy Las Vegas News Bureau.)

to other locations over the years, but its integrity was constantly preserved and its list of famous newlyweds grew to include Buck Owens, Mickey Rooney, Shirley Bassey, Richard Gere and Cindy Crawford, Zsa Zsa Gabor and George Sanders, Robert Goulet, Dudley Moore, Telly Sevalas, Mel Torme, Dinah Washington, and many, many others. As witness to its significance, the Little Church was listed on the National Registry of Historical Places in 1992. Ten years later, it celebrated its 60th anniversary at 3960 South Las Vegas Boulevard, enduring as the oldest existing structure on the Las Vegas Strip.

Griffith and Moore's Last Frontier also became a popular gathering spot for locals. For years, the hotel's spacious showroom offered the Hunt Breakfast, which was the forerunner of today's successful brunch buffets. It was an important part of many Las Vegans' Sunday morning routine to go to church and then gather for the sumptuous late-morning meal. The resort gained fame for its new entertainers, too, notably a 25-year-old, candelabra-carrying pianist named Walter Liberace, who made his debut there in 1944; Olympic swimmer Buster Crabbe who appeared in the hotel's Water Follies; and Sammy Davis Jr., who would settle at the Last Frontier for many years with the Will Mastin Trio after debuting in 1945 as its neighbor at the El Rancho.

On August 29, 1946, flush with cash from his business dealings and not to be outdone by competitors, Guy McAfee countered the openings of the Strip hotels by opening the Golden Nugget downtown. Along with partner Roscoe Thomas and attorney Artemus Ham Sr., McAfee's intention was to create "the brightest night spot in the world." Gaudy with neon lights, the Golden Nugget was the largest gambling hall in Las Vegas and it faced an equally glitzy casino—the Eldorado Club—which opened two days after the Nugget to replace the S.S. Rex Club. The retired Los Angeles police captain thus helped contribute yet another immutable nickname to the byways of Las Vegas, as the downtown area soon became referred to as "Glitter Gulch." The Golden Nugget was so immediately successful that its owners recouped their original investment in just nine months after opening.

Despite the beginnings of the Strip, downtown Las Vegas was still what exemplified the city to visitors and tourists in the mid-1940s. The city retained the image of a western town at the time. Visitors arriving by train were even greeted by a large sign saying, "Las Vegas—Still a Frontier Town," and the Wild West image was further confirmed by the opening of two local western wear shops by Rex Bell, husband of screen star Clara Bow. The stores advertised the "Las Vegas look"—custom-tailored cowboy suits, rhinestone-studded belts, shirts with snaps from cuff to elbow, and ten-gallon hats. Movie-star cowboys Joel McCrea, Tex Ritter, and Bob Steele were regular customers, adding credence to the authenticity of the image.

By 1946, however, a handful of savvy "boys from out East" were getting ready to challenge the California casino cronies and change that image forever—if not for good. Rumor had it that infamous Chicago mob boss Al Capone had set his sights on gaming operations in Reno and Las Vegas as early as 1931, but his arrest and imprisonment from 1932 to 1939 opened the way for other criminal gangs to take advantage of Nevada's liberalized gambling laws. As Prohibition was repealed and revenues from bootlegging dried up, crime syndicates saw ownership of casinos as a new cash cow. How right they would be.

Ten-year-old Mair Suchowljansky had fled Poland with his family in 1912 to avoid the Czarist Russian persecution of Jews. When he landed in New York City, he changed his name to Meyer Lansky. Over the next half-dozen years on the lower eastside of Manhattan, he grew streetwise and powerful, pulling together a gang of young cohorts who worked for the city's vice lords. Booze, heroin, prostitution, loan-sharking, extortion, bribery, money-laundering, hijacking, black-marketeering, murder . . . to Lansky, these were business opportunities, not crimes. Of all the businesses he could go into, however, gambling attracted him most. He didn't believe in luck; whoever controlled the game won, and "all the rest are suckers," he would say.

By the time he reached his 20s, Lansky and a boyhood friend, Sicilian immigrant Charles "Lucky" Luciano, had built a network of illegal casinos and speakeasy roadhouses that dotted the Eastern seaboard, extending west to Arkansas and as far south as Cuba. He ran his operations just like any other business, with specific revenue objectives, well-defined subsidiaries, profit-sharing for partners, bonus payments for "employees," and territories awarded to "managers" on the basis of geography, ethnicity, and performance. This network of organized crime became widely known as the "Syndicate."

Even in the 1920s, Lansky had considered setting up shop in Las Vegas, but he was dissuaded by the desert heat, calling the city "a horrible place" and "a small oasis town." When gambling was legalized in Nevada in 1931, he secretly acquired interest in Reno's Golden Casino and the Bank Club, at that time the state's largest gambling operation. As World War II got underway, he arranged to buy into Fremont Street properties—the Golden Nugget, Eldorado, and El Cortez—using partners like David "Davie" Berman, Moe Sedway, and Gus Greenbaum as his front men. Lansky himself maintained a low profile, preferring to have others work the front lines for him. One of those henchmen was a Brooklyn-born street chum, a man whose flair for flamboyance and slick sophistication, as well as his reputation for ruthlessness, would become synonymous with the Las Vegas Strip—Benjamin "Bugsy" Siegel.

Lansky had sent Siegel to Los Angeles in the early 1940s to take control of the wire there, the telegraph operations that communicated sports results to bookmakers across the country. Siegel found the California scene much to his liking, especially the glamour of Hollywood. He dressed in $300 suits, dined in the best restaurants with his flashy girlfriend, Virginia Hill, and hobnobbed with local glitterati, including Cary Grant, Jean Harlow, Jack Warner, Barbara Hutton, singer Kay Starr, and gangster-actor George Raft, who introduced him (unsuccessfully) to the stage. As the manager of local business, Siegel also had the power to arrange the death or disappearance of anyone who threatened the Syndicate's Los Angeles fiefdom. His teenage-earned nickname, which he hated, described his psychopathic temper perfectly: he was "crazy as a bedbug."

In 1941, Lansky wanted to expand race and sports betting operations to the downtown casinos of Las Vegas, so he put his old buddy Siegel and wire-man Moe Sedway in charge of investigating what business opportunities might be available on Fremont Street. This led to Sedway being assigned to run a new race book in the Turf Club at the Frontier, which he quickly leveraged into control of the wire at the Fremont Club and others. The Syndicate gradually claimed a virtual monopoly over all the major sports betting in the city. That caused smaller casino operators to protest all the way to the capital in Carson City, but state officials were so consumed with war-related activities, no action was taken to break the mob's cartel.

Meanwhile, impressed by Las Vegas, but not its casino center, Siegel felt more at home at the tables of the El Rancho and Last Frontier, and he soon became a frequent visitor to the Strip. It was during the time of these Las Vegas scouting missions and before the end of the war that the suave gangster came across another man whose tastes and vision he could easily relate to—William R. "Billy" Wilkerson, a popular Hollywood columnist, who had founded *The Hollywood Reporter* and three successful Los Angeles nightclubs: the Trocadero, Ciros, and La Rue.

Wilkerson had a dream of his own for Las Vegas. He wanted to create an amazing, completely different kind of hotel on the Strip, one based on the "swanky" clubs of Miami Beach and Beverly Hills. It would be a first-class pleasure palace, catering mainly to sophisticated clientele, the rich and famous, the high rollers. The hotel plans called for amenities unheard of at the time, including European-style bathrooms with bidets. Because Wilkerson happened to love exotic birds, it was probably his idea to call this resort the Flamingo, although history commonly gives Siegel that credit, naming it after the mascots of Florida's Hialeah Racetrack, or perhaps even a pet name for his mistress, the long-legged Virginia Hill. For a fact, it was Wilkerson who purchased the land for the project, near the future site of the county airport and far enough from the other two existing hotels to be had for a proverbial steal.

Wilkerson's dream had a flaw, however. War restrictions on building had prevented the construction of new hotels. Even afterwards, priority had to be given to erecting new industrial plants, civilian housing, and public works, not resorts. Building materials were in extremely short supply. What was available turned out to be very costly and for a truly posh luxury resort, there could be no shortcuts. As the nation's attention turned from war to peace, the Hollywood club-owner scrambled to bring his dream to reality, pouring an estimated $600,000 into the effort, but he ran out of cash and materials before the building could be completed. That's when Bugsy Siegel stepped in and made him an offer he couldn't refuse, raising $1 million in 1945 to buy Wilkerson out and get the fabulous Flamingo built.

As Siegel soon learned for himself, however, $1 million would not go very far on the Las Vegas Strip. He had his own adventurous ideas for the hotel, some of which were totally unrealistic as far as budget limits were concerned. For example, he had a special suite built for himself as a fourth-floor penthouse at the top of the three-story hotel behind the pool area. Besides being a glamorous apartment, it had all kinds of escape hatches, which Siegel felt he might need on short notice. He turned to Lansky and Luciano for more funds—first an additional million, then another two, and then more. He brought in Arizona-based Del Webb Corporation to finish the work. He was said to have invested up to $1 million of his own money in the development, plus nearly $6 million from his backers, but it still was not enough.

Theft may have been responsible for some of the cost overruns. Drivers of delivery trucks were said to bring construction materials in the front gate and then go right out the back without unloading. That might have accounted for some losses. Extravagance was to blame for others. To the original design, Siegel had added a health club and tennis courts, golf links, riding stables, landscaped lawns and gardens, palm trees, and a huge waterfall. But even that didn't seem to explain the project's final price tag of $6.5 million. Many in the Syndicate suspected their money might have been going elsewhere—such as Swiss bank accounts held by Virginia Hill, who made a number of trips to Europe during the period of construction. They began pressuring Siegel to open the resort and get revenues flowing.

Unfortunately, the Flamingo didn't start off with a bang, but as a big disappointment. Siegel insisted on holding the grand opening the day after Christmas, December 26, 1946. The timing was terrible. In those days, people did not vacation in Las Vegas over the Christmas holidays. What's more, the usually pleasant Las Vegas weather turned dreadfully wet and many of the invited guests decided to cancel.

Other unexpected problems occurred as well. The three-tiered fountain at the entrance of the hotel should have been a main feature, but someone discovered a cat and her baby kittens at the bottom of the fountain, which could not be removed. Instead of letting the small "first family" of the Flamingo come to an untimely end, Siegel decided to forego the water fountain display for the time being. (Whether he was truly a cat lover or just superstitious is not known, but it definitely put a halt to moving the feline family.) The entertainment was top-notch, featuring Jimmy Durante, George Jessel, Xavier Cugat, and Rose Marie, but the audiences were embarrassingly small and remained so throughout the ensuing week. On opening night, all the employees (including the janitors) dressed in tuxedos, which left the western-garbed locals wondering what to make of the place. They were insulted when asked to remove their cowboy hats. Then, as fortune would have it, some of the gamblers had amazingly good luck at the Flamingo's tables and the casino lost more than it took in on that first night.

To make matters worse, construction was still going on. The hotel rooms were not finished, so those guests who did come to stay had to be put up at competitors, the El Rancho and the Last Frontier. And as if the situation was not disastrous enough, unknown to Siegel, a meeting of Syndicate bosses had taken place in Havana the day before the opening. The owner's very life had been placed in the balance of the hotel's success or failure.

Lansky gave his old friend one last chance. Siegel was allowed to close the hotel two weeks after the opening and spend the next two months tying up all the loose ends. In March 1947, he gave it another go, relaunching the Flamingo with less fanfare, but bigger crowds. The casino-resort prospered into spring, but not with the level of financial success the Syndicate demanded. On June 20, 1947, Siegel was gunned down in Beverly Hills, while staying at Virginia Hill's Moorish-style mansion, by an assailant or assailants unknown. Hill was out of the country at the time. Within minutes after the murder, ownership of the Flamingo was claimed by the Syndicate's Phoenix-based casino specialist, Gus Greenbaum, who would later be credited with saving it, and fellow wise-guys Joe Rosenberg and Israel "Icepick Willie" Alderman.

The spectacular and grisly death of Siegel made headlines that would color the image of Las Vegas for decades to come. It also brought attention to the lawlessness that pervaded Nevada gambling. The Clark County seat went through six different police chiefs in the 1940s, none of them successful in stopping the rise in organized crime and some suspected of direct involvement in it. One even committed suicide only six days after taking office. Rules to regulate and tax gaming had been initiated in 1945, but little had been done to enforce them. Carson City legislators finally rose from their lethargy after Siegel's assassination in 1947 and enacted sweeping reforms, requiring state licensing of gaming operations and sports books and empowering the Nevada Tax Commission to investigate and monitor applicants. The following year, 11 Las Vegas race and sports book operators were ordered to appear before the tax authorities, which resulted in the suspension of licenses for Sedway and Alderman. Their later attempts to get the licenses reinstated were unsuccessful.

By then, however, the Syndicate was firmly in place on Fremont Street and the Strip. It would take more than slaps on the wrist to drive them away. And it would take more than a gangland hit to scare tourists away from their hotel-casinos. In fact, the notoriety of mob connections appealed to many people who visited Las Vegas. The city had always had a certain attraction to mavericks and outlaw wannabes. The criminal element was seen by many as an invitation to "come, live dangerously, take a chance." In a unique way, the Flamingo had essentially put Las Vegas on the map of the world. Apart from mob intrigues, it also had the distinction of being the world's first hotel constructed after World War II.

Visitors began coming to "Sin City" in droves. Crowds of more than 50,000 would gather to see the annual Helldorado parade, which from 1947 onward would be celebrated under the friendly gaze of a new city symbol introduced by the chamber of commerce—the "Howdy, Pardner" cowboy nicknamed Vegas Vic. More than a thousand Legionnaires would gather to hold their convention in the city. Couples getting unhitched in the town where 20-year-old Marilyn Monroe divorced first husband James Dougherty in September 1946 would flock to the new D-4-C ("divorcee") dude ranch opened by film star Hoot Gibson, the good-guy cowboy in the white hat. Travelers could still find the old-fashioned "western hospitality," but alongside it now was a new form of sophistication.

By 1947, the El Rancho Vegas had left Thomas Hull's hands and been picked up by Beldon Katleman, a crony of Guy McAfee, who pumped money into renovations, adding 220 rooms and a fresh French Provincial motif. Across the street, a classy new casino-nightclub opened, Club Bingo, a small 300-seat bingo parlor that would five years later evolve into the Sahara Hotel and Casino. The antes went up. The cash flowed faster. More high rollers came to town and more Hollywood "big names" arrived on the stages and in the audiences—including George "Gabby" Hays, Joe E. Lewis, Lena Horne, Bill "Bojangles" Robinson, and "the Voice" himself, Frank Sinatra. Although the city's oldest newspaper, the *Las Vegas Age*, closed its doors in 1947, new media organizations rose to take its place. To chronicle and promote all the excitement, the Las Vegas Press Club was organized, headed by first president Ray Germain, and the *Desert Sea* News Bureau (later the Las Vegas News Bureau) began photographing the city's star-studded entertainment scene.

Far from leaving what *Holiday Age* magazine had dubbed "the wildest Western city," the boys from the East increased their presence in Las Vegas, quietly buying into some operations and openly running others. As the 1940s rolled to a close, one more major hotel casino was added along Highway 91 with the Syndicate's blessings (and suspected backing): the Thunderbird. It was another case of spotting vacant land and having an idea for a new resort-casino. In this case, the visionaries were attorney Clifford Jones and developer Marion Hicks. The property was across the street diagonally from the El Rancho. The newest addition to the Strip was named after a mythical character from Navajo legend, meaning "sacred bearer of happiness unlimited." After the official opening was held on September 2, 1948, the Thunderbird soon became another popular place for tourists to visit. Especially attractive to the late-1940s in crowd was its intimate Joe's Oyster Bar. In an early brochure displaying a swimming pool ("the largest"), horseback riding, golf, a sample picture of one of the rooms, and of course, showgirls, the hotel described itself as "America's Most Luxurious Desert Hotel." No longer just a whistle stop on the way to some other destination, the Las Vegas that would take the stage in the second half of the twentieth century had arrived.

Chapter Five

THE EXPLOSIVE ERA

The 1950s started in Las Vegas with a boom as literal as it was figurative. Representing the big changes in the face of the city, a Life magazine photo-essay showed a mushroom cloud, appearing in the distance above the famous Fremont Street area, with Vegas Vic, the welcoming cowboy, smiling and waving just to the left of it. New atom bomb testing had begun in 1951 at Frenchman's Flat, also known as the Nevada Test Site, roughly 65 miles northwest of Las Vegas. The above-ground tests came to be social events, with locals getting up early to watch the blasts and hotels offering promotional viewings to visitors. Travel agents even provided guests with picnic lunches and transportation to a plateau where the explosions could be seen in all their splendor.

Making the most of the new tourist attraction, the Flamingo beauty parlor offered the latest, the Atomic Hairdo. The Sands staged a contest to choose Miss Atomic Bomb. And of course, one of the local bars had to create the Atomic Cocktail. For a while, makeshift communities were built near the testing, complete with mannequin citizens, as the military studied the effects of A-bomb blasts on civilian environments. The effects, of course, were devastating. Harm was done not only to the dummies, but to real live people and animals in the vicinity as well. Some military personnel stationed near the test site developed cancer in later life, although proving it was related to the open experimentation would be difficult.

At the time, most people were simply unaware of the horrific, long-lasting side-effects of the resultant radiation. Las Vegas residents were told by authorities how to "batten down the hatches" in their homes so that vases wouldn't break, but not about potential health risks. Apparently only a few were aware of such effects. The open explosions continued for more than a decade. Members of Non-violent Action Against Nuclear Weapons held a prayer vigil in 1957 and tried in vain to gain entry to the Nevada Test Site. Such protests did not meet with immediate success, but over time the public began to realize there were undisclosed dangers, and pressure mounted to stop the blasts. In 1962, the mushroom clouds finally disappeared. Thereafter, all the testing was moved underground.

Meanwhile, Las Vegas was becoming a major destination point for visitors for other reasons. The Lake Mead National Recreation Area alone attracted more than two million visitors by 1951. Hollywood movies, such as The Las Vegas Story starring Jane Russell, Victor Mature, and Vincent Price; and Meet Me in Las Vegas with Cyd Charisse and Dan Dailey, helped add to the allure of the city. To keep pace with the growing crowds of tourists, more new hotels were built and existing ones expanded. A variety of municipal improvements, befitting a fast-growing metropolitan area, were also added in short order, such as the first classes conducted by the University of Nevada, Las Vegas (UNLV) in 1951 and the opening of the city's first stand-alone public library in 1952 on the corner of Fourth and Mesquite, where the current city hall complex now stands.

In 1955, the Clark County Fair and Recreation Board was organized, forerunner of the current Las Vegas Convention and Visitors Authority (LVCVA). The group was charged with a dual mission: to attract visitors in support of local businesses, and to establish and operate a major convention center. The latter goal was realized four years later with the opening of a trade show complex, inaugurated by the World Congress of Flight and its 5,000 participants. Funds for the center's construction were appropriated by adding a tax to hotel and motel room charges, an assessment that directly benefited the owners of such accommodations through increased occupancy rates. In almost no time at all, Las Vegas became one of the major convention arenas in the United States and eventually the world.

Hotel construction reached an all-time high in the 1950s, with each new resort-casino intent on outdoing the previous one—being larger, better, offering more entertainment, more gambling choices, more delicious food, greater swimming pools, bigger name celebrities, and more beautiful showgirls. The results of this period of competition and expansion are still reflected in the monumental buildings that line the Las Vegas Strip today. The money that funded them, however, came from questionable sources. During the 1950s, nearly all the hotels that went up were financed, backed, or operated under mob influence.

The first major hotel added to the Strip line-up in the 1950s was the Desert Inn. It was the brainchild of Wilbur Clark, who was a living success story himself. He began as a bellman and then a bar owner in Los Angeles, later joining the migration of gamblers from California to Nevada in the late 1930s. Once in Las Vegas, Clark purchased an interest in the El Rancho Vegas and then built the Players Club on Highway 91. In 1945, he leased the city's first licensed downtown casino, the 1920 Northern Club, from Mayme Stocker and changed its name to the Monte Carlo Club.

Clark sold his shares in the El Rancho in 1946, purchased land across the street from the Last Frontier, and began construction on his dream, named after the Desert Inn Hotel in Palm Springs, which he admired. He lacked finances to complete the construction, however, so in 1949 he turned to backers in Cleveland and Detroit who had mob ties and illegal gambling backgrounds. One of them was former bootlegger Morris B. "Moe" Dalitz. Clark raised an estimated $4.5 million to realize his dream of a luxury-class oasis, complete with the city's first professional-quality golf course and rooms for high rollers that were in those days unmatched by the city's other properties.

When the Desert Inn opened on April 24, 1950, it was a resounding success. The featured performers in the showroom were Edgar Bergen and his wooden sidekick Charlie McCarthy. This act was soon followed by the Las Vegas stage debut of a headliner whose name would become almost synonymous with Las Vegas talent—Frank Sinatra. The hotel's 300 rooms were done in elegant Old West style and each featured individual thermostats, an innovation at the time. For years to come, it was known as "the class resort" on the Strip. In 1953, it was the first Las Vegas property to make sports a part of its appeal, hosting what would become the annual Tournament of Champions golf event at the Desert Inn Country Club.

Following right on Clark's heels, so to speak, was the Silver Slipper. This unique property could not rightfully be called a hotel, simply a casino, but it would become an important fixture in the annals of Las Vegas Strip history. It started as part of the Last Frontier Village, a recreated western town just north of the hotel and casino. New owner Beldon Katleman, who was also the El Rancho's proprietor, had wanted to call it the Silver Slipper from the very beginning, but the name was already being used by a small club on Boulder Highway. Katleman took care of that problem by buying the older property and then changing his new casino's temporary name of "Golden Slipper" back to his first choice in December 1950.

The Silver Slipper had the distinction of offering the city's first convention hall on its second story. It also featured great entertainment and was often frequented by stars such as Sinatra, who enjoyed being in the 2 a.m. audience after his own show at another hotel. The famous giant slipper that rotated in front of the building still exists, even though the building itself was torn down in 1988 (currently a parking lot); it is expected eventually to become part of the Neon Museum on Fremont Street.

Meanwhile, the downtown's Casino Center was continuing with its own expansion. Because it already had plenty of buildings, some standing since the town began in 1905, the new owners would continually remodel, expand, and rename the original properties. Among the structures lost to renovations were some of the city's most enduring landmarks. For example, the venerable Hotel Nevada, on the corner of Fremont Street and Main, continued under several different names and ownerships. In 1931, it became the Sal Sagev (Las Vegas spelled backwards) and, in 1957, it was purchased by a group of San Francisco entrepreneurs and renamed "The Golden Gate." One of its early claims to fame was its shrimp cocktails priced at 50¢, which are still available today for $1.

Benny Binion, another Las Vegas legend, came to Las Vegas in 1946. He had a dubious criminal past, mainly in Texas, and Las Vegas appeared to be the ideal place for him to start over. Binion purchased the Apache Hotel and the Eldorado Club beneath it. In August 1951, the combined properties officially opened as Binion's Horseshoe. It was reputedly the first downtown club to have carpeting on the floor and one of its big attractions was a Plexiglas horseshoe mounted near the casino entrance that displayed 100 brand-new $10,000 bills.

By all accounts, Binion was "one tough hombre." His nickname was "the Cowboy." Las Vegas newspaperman Dick Odessky has written, "He always carried a small pistol inside one of his custom-made cowboy boots, and stories have it that Benny racked up at least a dozen notches in his revolver handle even before leaving his native Texas in the 1940s."

One of those notches would have marked the 1931 murder of bootlegger Frank Bolding, for which Binion received a two-year suspended sentence. Another would have represented the self-defense shooting of a Texas numbers operator named Ben Frieden. The Cowboy served no jail time for the killings, but eventually, a brief prison stretch in the 1950s for tax evasion prohibited him from thereafter holding a Nevada gaming license. He had to turn over ownership of the Horseshoe to family members: sons Jack and Lonnie "Ted" Binion, serving as president and casino manager, respectively; their sisters Barbara, Brenda, and Becky, holding minority shares; and their mother Teddy Jane running the casino cage till her death in 1964. In no way, however, did the lack of a gaming license stop the ambitious Texan from leaving his imprint on the Las Vegas gambling scene.

Binion made waves with the owners of Strip casinos by constantly raising the limits on his table games. If their craps limit was $50, his would be $500. If their players could claim $270 on a single role of the dice, his could win up to $1,130. Nothing could curtail his competitive desire, not even the threat of death from alleged mob operatives, who saw these higher limits drawing action away from the tables they controlled. Eventually, limits on the Strip had to be raised to meet the Horseshoe's.

Among other Binion innovations were free limousine service to the airport for high rollers and free drinks for slot machine players, which would become staples among the offerings of all big Las Vegas casinos over the years. Binion and his boys also brought the World Series of Poker to the city, an annual event that still fills Casino Center hotels even today.

It was during this period of unbridled expansion that an ambitious young politician from Tennessee decided it was time to investigate the free-wheeling activities of the "boys from back East." Senator Estes Kefauver launched a study that brought him and his Washington crime committee to Las Vegas in November 1950. Over a two-day period, they called in witnesses and suspects to testify about their knowledge of "whether Las Vegas casino operators have any connections with nationwide Syndicates." Summoned to the hearings was Last Frontier architect Bill Moore, who by that time was head of the state tax commission. Moore shocked the investigators by challenging their right to interfere in Nevada's sovereign jurisdiction over its own gaming industry. He defended the state's grandfather clause that allowed people with backgrounds like Binion and Moe Sedway to own and run casino businesses. Unlike other states, where gaming operated illegally behind the backs of bribed officials, Nevada's gambling was out in the open, licensed and taxed under public control. Here it was legal and legitimate. As long as the Las Vegas casino owners broke no laws, why shouldn't they be allowed to pursue their business as they saw fit?

Kefauver's Senate Committee on Organized Crime was nonplussed as they heard similar testimony from Wilbur Clark of the Desert Inn, followed by then-Lieutenant

Governor Clifford Jones of the Thunderbird who told the same story. "As long as they conduct themselves properly," Jones said, "I think there is probably no harm in it." Into the next year, the investigators expanded their hearings to include questioning of Virginia Hill, Morris "Moe" Dalitz, and even Meyer Lansky himself, who risked charges of contempt of Congress by refusing to testify about his or Lucky Luciano's ties to Nevada casinos. In 1951, Kefauver issued his report. It was a bombshell, conclusively linking Syndicate money to Las Vegas casinos. The report was followed by a widely-sold book, *Crime in America*, and then the Tennessee senator proposed a 10-percent federal tax on all wagering and strict government control of licenses. The very thought of Washington's hands in their pockets brought shivers to the spines of mobsters and Las Vegas officials alike. Nevada politicians worked hard to defeat the measure, using all of Senator Pat McCarran's considerable influence to see that the proposal died in committee. Serious damage to Las Vegas and the Syndicate was averted. The building of new mob-funded casinos resumed—back to business as (un)usual.

On October 7, 1952, the five-year-old Club Bingo was reopened as the Sahara. Owner Milton Prell had it expanded to a full-size casino and hotel with an unusual North African desert theme. Its showroom featured headliner Lisa Kirk and dancer Ray Bolger, best known for his role as the Scarecrow in the film version of *The Wizard of Oz*. A year later, the hotel would showcase film star and chanteuse Marlene Dietrich on stage, paying her the unheard of sum of $30,000 weekly. The Sahara also had one of the Strip's first popular lounges, the Casbar theater, which really made waves when former New Orleans trumpeter Louis Prima, his wife singer Keely Smith, and Sam Butera and the Witnesses opened there for a long run in late 1954. Soon, it was standing room only for "the wildest show" in Las Vegas.

Lounge talent in the mid-1950s also included singing acts like the Treniers (still active into the twenty-first century), Freddie Bell and the Bellboys, and "Hi-dee-ho" Cab Calloway. Until Prima and Smith hit town, however, lounge acts were not casino stock and trade. Their most successful predecessor was probably the Mary Kaye Trio, composed of brother and sister Norman and Mary Kaye, who were of Hawaiian descent, though raised in Missouri. Their third partner was a comedian named Frank Ross, whose wacky improvisations predated those of comedians Don Rickles and Shecky Greene. For 22 straight weeks until 1954, the three performed the graveyard shift from midnight until dawn in the Last Frontier's lounge, attracting crowds of visiting insomniacs, sleepless gamblers, bus boys, off-duty showgirls, and even big-name entertainers—Milton Berle, Red Skelton, and Phil Silvers among them. Las Vegas was learning to rock around the clock. Lounge hopping would become a favorite form of entertainment over the next 15 years.

In 1952, another Syndicate-financed Strip casino opened with a desert theme— the Sands. Owner-builder Jake Friedman had come to Las Vegas, intent on building a luxury hotel. He purchased the LaRue Restaurant on Highway 91 and began construction on that property in early 1952. The naming of the Sands is a classic Las Vegas story. Reportedly, Friedman had intended to name his hotel the Holiday Inn after a successful 1942 movie starring Bing Crosby and Fred Astaire. One day on the construction lot, however, Friedman complained about all the "damned sand" in his shoes. He sarcastically said his property should be named "The Sand." Someone else took it one step further and said, "No, it should be plural: The Sands." The name stuck.

The grand opening on December 15 featured entertainers Danny Thomas, Billy Eckstine, and Jane Powell. One of Friedman's partners, Jack Entratter, was formerly with the Copacabana Nightclub in New York. He brought his expertise and show-biz connections along with him to the Sands, creating the Copa Room, which for years to come would be the location of memorable performances in its intimate atmosphere, where the stage entertainers could, and often would, mingle with the audience. The Copa Girls, the Sands' own prestigious showgirls, were advertised as "the most beautiful girls in the world" and were envied by their counterparts in the other properties.

The other name that would become synonymous with the Sands (and Las Vegas) was that of Frank Sinatra. Entertainment's original "ol' blue eyes," Sinatra had been a bobby-soxer idol at the Paramount Theatre in New York City in the early 1940s and was most likely the nation's first true "teen idol." By the early 1950s, however, Sinatra started to lose some of his luster. Two events happened to turn his luck around: an Oscar-winning performance as Maggio in the film *From Here to Eternity* and his live performances at the Sands, which demonstrated his more mature, more knowing attitude, and a voice better than ever. By 1953, he had scandalized the public with his divorce from his wife Nancy, in his pursuit of gorgeous film star Ava Gardner. Their match was tumultuous and short-lived and Sinatra ended up returning to Vegas to nurse his wounds, a sadder but wiser man. His affiliation with the Sands was a success for both the hotel and Sinatra. Jack Entratter wisely gave the crooner a "piece of the action" (a percentage of the hotel's profits), so Sinatra was, in essence, part owner of the Sands. The comeback-minded star liked to gamble, too. Some biographers state that the hotel allowed Sinatra to keep his winnings and tore up his markers for his losses. Others say that it was more likely he was just "shilling," pretending to play with his own money, but it really belonged to the house, so he didn't actually win or lose.

On stage, Sinatra was a crowd pleaser and he drew other entertainers like a magnet—joining him to perform or sitting front row in his audience. It was not uncommon to see screen stars such as Gary Cooper, Spencer Tracy, Lucille Ball, and others in the crowd. Nor was it unusual for Sinatra to visit the other acts in town for his own entertainment. This is how he became familiar with fellow Las Vegas performers Sammy Davis Jr. and Dean Martin—the beginnings of the incredible Rat Pack.

Sinatra's new troupe, which was soon joined by comedian Joey Bishop and actor Peter Lawford, was at first called The Clan, but unwanted connotations of the Ku Klux Klan caused them switch to the new and improved Rat Pack. Their name was taken from The Holmby Hills Rat Pack of Hollywood, originally, which included luminaries and buddies Humphrey Bogart, Lauren Bacall, Judy Garland, and Sinatra, among others. Clowning around on the Sands stage with cigarettes lit and glasses of booze in hand, they were the toast of the town. Sinatra was their recognized Chairman of the Board.

The Rat Pack hit its peak when the entertainers were brought together to star in the now classic film *Oceans 11*. The movie is enduring not only because of the merriment, drama, and merging of such talented performers, but also for its freeze-frame images of the Las Vegas Strip as it was in 1960. The film included several "new Rats"—Angie Dickinson, Shirley MacLaine, and Caesar Romero, among others—and it starred five major Strip hotel-casinos: The Sands, Flamingo, Desert Inn, Sahara, and the Riviera.

The filming of the movie was a magical time for Las Vegas. The Rat Pack would shoot their scenes in the day time, then perform on stage at night. Audiences would never know who was going to show up. In fact, the Sands showroom poster at the time displayed a picture of each performer, Sinatra, Martin, Davis, Lawford, and Bishop, and in the center stated, "Star light, star bright, which star shines tonight?" Even the management didn't know and the evenings were much more fun that way. There would usually be at least three of the stars on stage, often all five of them. Sometimes Sinatra would be the star, sometimes Martin. Whoever stole center stage, their show always guaranteed mayhem, improvisation, great tunes, and even cake fights at times. "Anything goes" was their motto, which is exactly how it went.

Those were truly the glory days for Sinatra and friends—and Las Vegas, too, which adopted them as its unofficial ambassadors. It was an era of being "cool," ring-a-ding-ding, martinis, chain smoking, spontaneous wit, and beautiful women, never to be repeated. It was also the eve of Camelot in Washington, D.C. and a young politician joined the Sands audience to applaud the Pack, Peter Lawford's brother-in-law, John F. Kennedy. Sinatra took an instant liking to Kennedy and actively campaigned for his election to the Presidency. In 1971, Sinatra would take a three-year break from the stages of Las Vegas and retire to his Palm Springs home. In 1978, he'd be feted at the biggest star-studded party ever thrown on the Strip, a tribute to his 64th birthday and 40 years as a recording artist. Later stage appearances kept the Rat Pack's Chairman of the Board in the public eye and Las Vegas's heart until his death in 1998.

As Sinatra launched on his upward trajectory, the Syndicate continued along theirs. In 1954, mob money headed off the Strip to pick up on a dream that had failed Tony Cornero a decade earlier, on Fremont Street where it meets Boulder Highway. The Showboat (initially named the Desert Showboat Motor-Hotel) was designed to resemble a Mississippi Riverboat, with a décor of highly polished woodwork and ornate and richly-colored red, white, and gold wallpaper, reminiscent of the 1870s. Opened by Bill Moore, J. Kell Houssels, and Joe Kelley on September 3, 1954, it was billed as "Las Vegas's first resort hotel," which was technically true, since all the resort hotels on "The Strip" were outside the Las Vegas city limits proper. It also was the first of the big hotel-casinos to target the local population, rather than out-of-towners, as its customer base. Ten gallons of water sent by the St. Louis Chamber of Commerce were used to christen the landlocked ship. Pop Squires, former editor of the *Las Vegas Age*, and his wife performed the honors. Among headline acts featured at the Showboat's expansive Mardi Gras Room was an original burlesque show, Minsky's Follies of 1955.

Apart from its off-track location and target market, the hotel was unique in other ways, too. It was one of the first Vegas properties to sponsor bus tours from southern California and Arizona. It was also the first hotel to contain a bowling alley of 24 lanes, which opened in 1959. The following year, the Showboat would sign a contract with the Pro Bowlers Association, making it the nationally televised home of the annual Las Vegas Open. Among other breaks from tradition were the addition of a permanent bingo room, a professionally staffed Kiddies Playroom, and a showroom with no cover or minimum charge.

It seemed that city and county authorities had turned a blind eye to mob activity after surviving Kefauver's crime-busting scrutiny. In fact, businessmen from both sides of the street found mutual benefit in cooperation. It was often said that Las Vegas had two police forces: one paid out of municipal accounts and one funded by the gangsters. At times, they could be one and the same. Neither group wanted any trouble and certainly not any incidents that might cause headlines or investigations. The word was out, even among wiseguys, "If you want to be stupid, don't do it in Las Vegas. Keep the city clean." Longtime residents sometimes refer wistfully to this time of peace and relative safety. With deadly criminals in charge of keeping order, no one dared rob, assault, or murder anyone—without permission, at least.

If the mob and local politicians had an enemy in town in those days, it was the press. The city's most powerful media man was newspaper editor Henry M. "Hank" Greenspun, a former lawyer who had been the publicity director of the Flamingo under Bugsy Siegel in 1947. He had also worked for Wilbur Clark at the Desert Inn, and he knew the inner workings of the Syndicate and county-city government as well as anyone. In 1950, Greenspun bought out a local tri-weekly, the *Las Vegas Free Press*, and turned it into a daily named the *Las Vegas Sun*. Throughout the 1950s and 1960s, he would ferret out criminals wherever they hid and reveal their activities to the public. He defined the newspaper's mission to "always fight for progress and reform" and "never tolerate injustice or corruption." In 1954, Greenspun bravely exposed the brothel ownership of Clark County Sheriff Glen Jones. The paper's muckraking led to the resignation of Lieutenant Governor Clifford Jones as the state's national committeeman for the Democratic Party. The newsman even went after the mob, which may have caused the *Sun's* offices to be torched in 1963. Labor racketeer Tom Hanley was suspected of setting the blaze, although fire officials blamed it on spontaneous combustion, not arson.

About the only time local government and the Syndicate crossed swords was over who got to keep a bigger piece of the gambling revenue pie. The Strip casinos were in Clark County territory, outside the Las Vegas city limits. If the city's boundaries could be extended south to the airport, municipal tax revenues would zoom, providing the money needed to pay down accumulating debt and pay for new public works projects. In 1950, Mayor Ernie Cragin proposed annexation to capture the Strip's tax base—not a plan the prospering hotel-casino owners took lightly. They thwarted Cragin by getting the county to give their properties the status of an unincorporated township on December 8, 1950. They named it Paradise City. Under Nevada law, incorporated cities cannot annex an unincorporated township without approval from the county commissioners. Unwilling to let their own cash cow go, the Clark County officials would never let that happen.

In 1951, Cragin turned to extortion to get his way. He threatened to turn off the supply of sewerage services to the Thunderbird, El Rancho, and Bingo Club unless they capitulated. The casinos called his bluff and neither a takeover nor a shutdown occurred. The Syndicate simply let Clark County officials do their fighting for them. Before long, unincorporated townships would spring up all around Las Vegas City, blocking municipal expansion and clearly defining whose turf was whose.

If the 1950s marriage of gang and government seemed strange, what then to make of an even odder pair of bedfellows—the Mob and the Mormons? The Latter-Day Saints prohibited their members from gambling. Even participation in the 1905 Las Vegas auction had been forbidden as a form of speculation. When gaming was legalized in 1931, church leaders in Utah shook their heads; Las Vegas was a false economy being built on gambling and hedonism. But financier E. Parry Thomas, a non-practicing Mormon, saw a loophole in church rules. Direct participation in ventures of vice might be taboo, but that shouldn't include investment by non-LDS members in casino construction.

Thomas had been sent to Las Vegas by Salt Lake City's Continental Bank in 1954 to establish the Bank of Las Vegas. Thomas's Utah boss, Walter Cosgriff (a Catholic), had made profits on construction loans to Del Webb Corporation in the development of the Flamingo in the 1940s. Taking a page from Cosgriff's playbook, the Mormon banker came up with a plan to channel funds from the Teamster Union's Central State Pensions Fund into Las Vegas resort building projects. It wasn't Mormon money. Thomas claimed no ownership in the casinos. His bank could earn profits from the Strip's explosive growth nonetheless. Moreover, the casinos paid back faithfully and offered the nation's top dollar in interest. It was a win-win situation for everyone, including future pensioners. Within a year after opening, the Bank of Las Vegas lent $15 million to gaming operators. Before federal authorities would step in and turn off the flow of union monies, Thomas was able to move $230 million worth of pension funds into new casinos. He was promoted to the bank's presidency in 1959.

If church officials were less than pleased with this situation, casino owners couldn't have been happier. The involvement of a legitimate lending institution and such an upright citizen as Thomas was great for their image, as well as their development budgets. The Las Vegas Resort Hotel Association tried to make donations to support local LDS operations, but the First Presidency in Salt Lake City ordered the "tainted" money returned. Someone had to draw the line. As the years moved on, though, that line would become increasingly blurry. Together with a Jewish partner, Jerome "Jerry" Mack, and under the blessing of Teamster Union leader Jimmy Hoffa, Thomas bankrolled facelifts and construction for a dozen or more Syndicate-owned properties through the early 1960s.

On April 21, 1955, the next pleasure palace to debut in "Paradise City" on Highway 91 (Las Vegas Boulevard) was the Riviera, opening at a cost of $8.5 million. The Riviera had the distinction of having the first high-rise on the Strip—a tower with nine stories. At the time, there was some concern about whether the porous desert land could support a tower as tall as this, but much taller structures would follow. Its décor was designed to replicate the French Riviera; even the doormen reflected this motif, garbed in French Foreign Legion uniforms. To lure gamblers, its opening act was the hottest talent around, pianist Liberace, who was paid an outrageous salary of $50,000 a week.

Liberace had been lured over to the new property from the Last Frontier, where he had previously performed. During that same period, a newcomer to the music business, Elvis Presley, was appearing at the Last Frontier. In a publicity shot at the time, Presley donned Liberace's sparkling jacket and Liberace wore Presley's "cool" jacket. Interestingly, the young singer was a flop during his first Las Vegas stint. However, when he returned and made a major comeback in 1969, his jumpsuits were encrusted in jewels, much like Liberace's.

The Riviera had money from several Miami investors, who apparently did not know much about operating a hotel. It filed for bankruptcy after only three months. The Syndicate called in Gus Greenbaum, formerly of the Flamingo, to save it. He did and stayed until 1958 when illness forced him to move back to his home in Arizona. A few months later, on December 3, 1958, Greenbaum and his wife were murdered mob-style in their desert home. The murders were never solved, although there is a strong belief that he was hit by his own gangland family, probably because of the massive amount of money he owed them, due to his gambling and drug use excesses.

In the 1960s and after, the hotel's Versailles Showroom hosted some of the nation's top entertainers—Mitzi Gaynor, Dean Martin, Carol Channing, Debbie Reynolds, and Merv Griffin, to name but a few. With its intimate Starlite Theater Lounge, gourmet-class Delmonico restaurant, 300-seat Café Noir coffee shop, and some 770 elegant rooms and suites, the Riviera certainly deserved its moniker as the "Flagship" of the luxurious Las Vegas resorts.

Only five years into the decade, 1950s Las Vegas was already awash with newly built casinos, but there would be more. The downtown district's response to the Riviera high-rise was the Fremont Hotel, with a 15-story tower, Nevada's tallest building at the time. Ed Levinson, who had previous success as a hotelier in Miami, was the brains behind the huge $6-million, 155-room building. Its opening in May 1956 attracted not only media attention, but media tenants as well, with the Las Vegas Press Club and future ABC-TV affiliate KSHO-TV moving their offices into the tower to take advantage of its height for broadcast transmitters. It was also the perfect venue for A-bomb test viewing, but the hotel would become best known for its outstanding food at great prices and the equally outstanding entertainment in its Carnival Lounge.

About this time, a young singer named Wayne Newton got his start at the Fremont, along with his brother Jerry and their group called The Jets. Newton was then a teenager and too young to even walk through the casino. It was said he spent his off-time at the drugstore soda fountain across the street. After splitting up with brother Jerry, Newton would become a full-fledged star on his own. His first hit record, *Danke Schoen*, sold millions worldwide in 1963. Thereafter, he continued to perform in Las Vegas and had a short stint at ownership of the Aladdin Hotel. Although Newton headlined and owned a property in Branson, Missouri for a time, his primary home was his well-known Las Vegas estate, Casa de Shenendoah. Notching his 25,000th performace in 1996, Newton continues to appear nightly in his own theater at the Stardust Hotel. In addition to charity work and numerous citizenship awards, he managed to have enough spare time to win an international award for his most active hobby, the breeding of Arabian horses.

Another perennial star who got his start in mid-century Las Vegas was Jerry Lewis. He was half of the wildly popular "Martin and Lewis" act with Dean Martin and they appeared frequently in the showrooms in Las Vegas. In fact, their first movie, *My Friend Irma Goes West*, featured Las Vegas and the Flamingo Hotel as a background for their crazy antics. Once the team split up, both entertainers gained solid success on their own. Lewis went on to star in and direct many films. He has headed up the Muscular Dystrophy Association's yearly telethon for over 30 years. After the telethon moved from New York to Las Vegas in the early 1970s, the live telecast was based at the Sahara Hotel and Convention Center. Lewis continues to maintain a home in Las Vegas, still performs on stage, and is one of the city's many celebrity citizens.

As if two desert-theme resorts were not enough on the Strip, on May 23, 1955, the 200-room Dunes opened with Vera-Ellen, popular actress and dancer, starring in the showroom and heading up the Magic Carpet Review. Unlike the Riviera, the Dunes reverted to the earlier popular Strip style of low-rise motel-like buildings surrounding a huge Olympic-sized pool. At the time, it was the southernmost property on the Strip, situated where the Bellagio stands today. The Dunes' signature look was embodied by a 30-foot-tall, beaming sultan perched atop the entrance and designed by YESCO.

Probably because of the proliferation of hotels in Las Vegas at the time, combined with poor management, the Dunes closed its doors after only one year. In true Las Vegas fashion, however, it reemerged a month later, re-opened under new management in June 1956. Its new show was Minsky's Follies, shanghaied from the Showboat, given a burlesque flavor, and choreographed with a new dance innovation; it became the first major act on the Strip to feature bare-bosomed female performers. Over the decade that followed, the Dunes would expand its capacity by 800 rooms with a 21-story high-rise tower, while adding a huge ballroom, an 18-hole golf course, an Alice-in-Wonderland nursery, and what Diners Club would name "America's finest and most beautiful restaurant," the 170-seat Sultan's Table. Patrons of the restaurant were entertained nightly by Arturo Romero and his Magic Violins.

The Dunes' reign as the Strip's southernmost hotel ended the same month it reopened, when the Hacienda Hotel and Casino commenced business operations in June 1956. In its planning stages, it was called The Lady Luck, but it was eventually renamed the Hacienda after other hotels in California with the same name, all owned and operated by Warren "Doc" Bayley. Since it was extremely isolated and located across the street from McCarran Airport, the Hacienda tried to attract visitors as they approached Las Vegas from the southwest. It was not the fanciest of Strip casinos. It even gained the nickname "Hayseed Heaven" because it catered to families and had no showroom. It did, however, have two swimming pools and a go-kart race track for the kids.

Suffering through some hard times in its early months, the Hacienda management decided that someone should stand at a busy intersection in Barstow, California, and hand out promotional flyers to the drivers of cars who were stalled there during the construction of the expanding highway to Las Vegas. This marketing tactic was so successful that the idea was taken one step further by hiring two attractive cocktail waitresses to pass out the flyers. Another brainstorm was the creation of "junket trips" for gamblers—bringing in high rollers from California on free flights, with complimentary rooms and free meals, while they gambled their money away. This was a time of tough competition among casinos in Las Vegas and hotels had to begin doing more than just open with big name acts. They had to have a gimmick.

In time, Doc Bayley would pass ownership of the Hacienda on to his wife Judy, who became known in local circles as the city's "First Lady of Gambling." Female entrepreneurs were rare enough in the 1950s and 1960s, but a woman heading up a sprawling multimillion-dollar gaming casino and hotel complex was something rare even in Las Vegas.

A resort of a very different type made its Strip debut on April 4, 1957—the beautiful $18-million Tropicana. It was soon dubbed the "Tiffany of the Strip." Its centerpiece roadside attraction was a 60-foot-high tulip fountain that glowed in shades of rose and aqua at night. Over $1 million was spent on the resort's landscaping alone. It was, at the time, the classiest joint on the Strip, evoking much of its atmosphere from the beautiful showplace hotels in Miami and reminiscent of Old Havana. The Tropicana was the creation of Ben Jaffe, who headed the Fontainebleu Hotel in Miami Beach. It was said that it was constructed with the idea of it being a luxury hotel first and a gambling establishment second. Even the rooms could be entered without going through the casino, which at the time was not de rigeur.

Due to a combination of mob connections and ostentatious (some called it unfriendly) management, the Tropicana resort began to have problems. This was resolved by bringing in J. Kell Houssels, longtime Las Vegas businessman and part-owner of the El Cortez and Showboat, who began shifting the ambience of the hotel and turned it into a very people-friendly place. Like the Desert Inn, they built a golf course, a first-class, 18-hole, par-70 venue across the street (where the MGM Grand stands now). It offered a beautiful Olympic-sized pool with a fountain in the center, surrounded by palm trees and tropical flora and fauna. There were also several night-lighted tennis courts, which hotel guests could use free of charge. Later, in 1959, the Trop's entertainment director, Lou Walters (father of television journalist Barbara Walters), was instrumental in bringing the renowned Folies Bergere from Europe to Las Vegas at an estimated cost of $800,000. Today, it is one of the Strip's longest-running shows and continues to be a major must-see attraction.

Perhaps it is fitting that the wild building spree on the Strip ended in the 1950s with a contribution from the man who had dreamt of such luxurious Las Vegas clubs nearly two decades earlier. Tony Cornero, the gambler and gangster who had failed with the Meadows in the 1930s and abandoned the S.S. Rex Club in the 1940s, was back for one more round. His goal this time was to create the biggest and best hotel and casino on the Strip to date. He called it the Stardust.

Cornero purchased 32 acres of Strip property for $650,000. It would have been a storybook ending for the admiral if he had succeeded. But on July 31, 1955, well before construction was complete, Cornero died while throwing dice at a Desert Inn craps table. Unsubstantiated rumors still persist whether he might have injected or been injected with a drug in the hotel bathroom on the night he passed away.

Cornero's dream did not die with him, however. John "Jake the Barber" Factor, brother of famous Hollywood makeup artist Max Factor, came up with funds to complete the Stardust, although he too would run into financial problems. That led to the intervention of Moe Dalitz and the "boys," who took over construction of the Stardust with money invested by the Teamster's Union in 1958. Dalitz, "the toughest Jewish mobster in Las Vegas," would also lead the group that obtained the Desert Inn from Wilbur Clark in 1962.

In typical Las Vegas grandiose style, on July 2, 1958, the long-awaited Stardust opened with 1,000 rooms as the largest hotel casino in the world. It also boasted the largest neon marquee ever seen—once again, designed by YESCO—measuring 27 feet tall and stretching across 216 feet in the front of the resort. The sign was a mind-boggling concoction of planets, moons, and stars in multicolor splendor. It could be seen from more than 3 miles away.

The Stardust showroom was larger than a basketball court and had the distinction of offering the first French-import show, the Lido de Paris. What's more, some of the showgirls were topless, which caused quite a stir. Topless revues introduced previously used "pasties" to cover dancers' nipples; the Stardust's showgirls were completely bare-breasted. However, the end result was a top-class production under the leadership of now-legendary Donn Arden and its performances always sold out, right from the beginning.

The Stardust enveloped a smaller hotel which had gone under, the $5-million Royal Nevada. This property, by default, became the hotel's convention center. It also gained through this incorporation a second swimming pool, which is today the only original Strip pool remaining. The Stardust offered its guests much besides the traditional hotel and casino amenities. It boasted a rodeo arena and even a drive in movie theatre on the property, which grew quite popular by showing "all-night, continuous movies."

This was to be the last of the grand hotels along the Strip to be opened in the 1950s. In fact, there was almost a standstill in construction until the mid-1960s. One reason for the stoppage was the glut of competing rooms; another was Governor Charles Russell's 1955 to 1957 development of an elaborate system to tax casinos. Taxation and licensing was overseen by a new bureau of highly trained investigators and accountants to check on gambling operations—the Gaming Control Board. The board was still not a big threat to mob interests, but they did manage to shut down the Thunderbird temporarily for violations of ownership regulations. They also delayed the opening of the Hacienda by refusing to license the appointed casino manager, Jake Kozloff, who was suspected of Syndicate ties.

Many of the other gambling facilities that did manage to open before the turndown had short lifespans. Two Vegas landmarks were lost to fires—the Boulder Club in 1956 and the original El Rancho Vegas on July 17, 1960. Mercifully, there were no fatalities in the El Rancho blaze, but it marked the death of an era. Several years later, George Stamos of the Las Vegas Sun wrote eloquently about the event:

> Many wept that morning, because the El Rancho symbolized so many things about this town: its friendliness, its openness, the glamour of top stars, and above all, the pioneer spirit of the first major investors in Las Vegas' gaming future. It took only an hour for the flames to destroy what for 20 years had stood as the epitomy [sic] of the Las Vegas resort industry.
>
> Now the El Rancho property sits vacant, a forlorn and weed-infested monument to what was once the colorful and lively first great resort in a long

line of dazzling Strip establishments. Parts of the remaining structures on the acreage were carted off to "Old Vegas" (now West World), the Old West amusement park outside of Henderson. The rest of the buildings crumble under the hot desert sun.

Where once starlets frolicked and Eastern cowboys flirted with Dame Fortune, now lizards and tumbleweeds cavort and play. Few newcomers to Las Vegas are aware of the importance that piece of vacant land once held. But those who lived here when the Queen still reigned supreme in the early days of the Strip will affectionately recall the Western grace and splendor.

El Rancho Vegas was the first, and she will never be forgotten.

In the midst of the building boom and grand openings of casinos along the Strip, one other daring construction experiment was taking place on the Westside of Las Vegas. Much as it may have needed it in some ways, this project did not receive mob help—the creation of the Moulin Rouge.

By the 1950s, Las Vegas had gained two conflicting reputations. Among many Americans, it was thought of as the "Black Entertainment Capital of the World," owing to the many African Americans who performed on its stages. To those who really understood the local social scene, however, it was more appropriately the "Mississippi of the West." Apart from a few towns in the Deep South, Las Vegas had become one of the most segregated places in the country. Even though the casinos had long featured famous black performers in their showrooms—from Lena Horne and Dorothy Dandridge to Lionel Hampton, Louis Armstrong, Red Foxx, Pearl Bailey, and Eddie "Rochester" Anderson (Jack Benny's sidekick)—the sad truth was they were not allowed to stay in the rooms or play in the gambling areas. They were forced to rent rooms on the Westside at boarding houses "run by their own kind." Nat "King" Cole was reportedly "disgusted and dismayed" at being able to star in a hotel, but unable to eat or sleep there—or even to look around its casino. Like other African-American entertainers, Cole had to stay in West Las Vegas where, astonishingly, rooming house owners took advantage of the out-of-town guests. The performers were suspected of being wealthy by virtue of their stylish profession, so the room keepers charged them higher fees than they did their regular boarders.

The Moulin Rouge was to change all that as the first interracial hotel-club in Las Vegas, a $3.5-million resort built on land owned by Will Max Schwartz with the backing of New York restaurateur Louis Reuben and Los Angeles broker Alexander Bismo, among several partners. The daringness of this concept can hardly be overstated. Even Sammy Davis Jr., unquestionably the most popular black entertainer in Las Vegas, who broke color barriers everywhere, called the Westside "the Las Vegas version of Tobacco Road." It was a ghetto, a slum, where as many as 16,000 African Americans and other "coloreds" were resident. The notion of white patrons joining African Americans and Hispanics in a Westside club of any scale was nigh on unthinkable. Only true visionaries, who could see beyond prejudice to the tremendous profits to be had in opening gambling and entertainment to all races, could possibly have dreamed up the Moulin Rouge.

Opening on May 24, 1955, the interracial hotel-club seemed poised for greatness. It quickly became the after-hours hangout for most of the stage stars, both black and white, who were appearing in the Las Vegas showrooms. Observers widely agreed that the Strip hotels had some stiff competition with the new resort. It was a first-class joint with top entertainment throughout the night until the wee hours. The Moulin Rouge had achieved its brief but shining moment in the entertainment and political history of Las Vegas, but Schwartz and his partners soon had a falling out over money. They had underestimated the financing and management skill needed to make the dream work. Within seven months, the Moulin Rouge was closed, bankrupt.

In his oral history, Fighting Back, civil rights activist James B. McMillan recalls getting married at the original nightclub in 1957:

> Ed Sullivan happened to be in the Moulin Rouge at the time, and Billy Daniels sang the wedding song for us. These people were there just for the entertainment. That was the only integrated hotel in town at that time, and all of these people . . . (Barbara) Hutton, the wealthy heiress, was there. And when we had the wedding, all these people just came out and had a party. . . . When the hotel closed a few months later it was not because of not having any business; it closed because the partners just couldn't get along and they decided not to pay any more bills.

Unpaid building contractors demanded their money. Negotiations with creditors lasted for over a year while the building filled with dust. In 1957, developer Leo Fry bought the hotel and reopened it, but the relaunched property would endure only three more years. Ironically, its demise was brought about by the NAACP. They filed law suits against Fry, who happened to be white, for charging his white customers less for drinks than his black patrons. Two suspensions of the Moulin Rouge liquor license resulted; sit ins and demonstrations were threatened. Eventually, Fry gave up and shut the hotel in 1960.

For more than four decades, the Moulin Rouge waited patiently for revival. It was included on the National Register of Historic Places in 1992, and its restoration was proposed time and again. Then, on May 29, 2003, a fast-moving, three-alarm fire destroyed the famous old building, leaving only its marquee standing intact. Owner Bart Maybie has indicated that some of the $2 million received in insurance may be used to rebuild the structure in time for a 50th anniversary celebration in May 2005, but the original Moulin Rouge is now gone forever.

In the wake of the Moulin Rouge's failure to desegregate the Las Vegas entertainment scene, white patrons had to return to Fremont Street and the Strip, while non-white customers went back to the Westside's own establishments, such as the El Rio, the Town Tavern, and the Louisiana Club. These did good business, if only because their clientele was restricted from going elsewhere. Bitterness grew among the area's minority residents. The Syndicate's hotel-casinos were not open to African Americans, but their dirty work was. Housekeeping staff of the Flamingo and downtown hotels were predominantly black. They could be the cooks and dishwashers of the city's restaurants, but not their customers. The Moulin Rouge became a symbol of their outrage over bigotry. It also gave them a forum for protest.

The call for civil rights grew louder as the 1960s approached. Even Sammy Davis Jr., who seemed beyond color and had even claimed Las Vegas as his "spiritual home," could feel the race hatred and local discrimination, although he never let it defeat him. He would later joke, "Long before there was a civil rights movement, I was marching through the lobby of the Waldorf Astoria, of the Sands, the Fountainbleau, to a table at the Copa. I'd marched alone."

In December 1954, Davis was involved in a traumatic and almost fatal car accident in San Bernardino, California, en route from Las Vegas to Los Angeles. He lost his left eye in the crash. At that time, his Rat Pack buddy Frank Sinatra visited the hospital and assured him, "Relax. You're going to be bigger than ever, Charley. Bigger than ever." That prophecy would prove true. Jack Entratter signed him to a long-term contract at the Sands. He would play Las Vegas for as long as there was a stage there and an audience to appreciate him. He would also be around to see the city gradually turn color blind. Davis died of cancer in 1990, but his Las Vegas legend lives on, memorialized in an amphitheatre named after him in Lorenzi Park.

All minority groups suffered the effects of racial prejudice and segregation at this time. In the 1950s, the Hispanic population of Las Vegas declined from 2,275 at the start of the decade to a mere 236 at its close, even though the city's black component grew to 9,649 and the white population more than doubled to 54,261 during the same period. Where racial pressure brought the city's African Americans together in opposition, it caused the majority of the area's Hispanics to pack up and simply move away. Many of them, in fact, were driven out.

In 1954 and 1955, the federal government launched a nationwide purge of undocumented Mexicans: Operation Wetback. Instructing the Immigration and Naturalization Service to find, round up, and deport illegal workers, this overtly cruel program traumatized Mexican-American communities throughout the Southwest. Many of their members had come north since 1942 as *braceros*—farm hands and railroad workers needed to fill the labor shortage caused by World War II. Now that the country was at peace and had its own citizens to employ, the guest workers were no longer welcome. Not surprisingly, many chose to leave on their own, rather than be forced out.

Of the Hispanics who did gain from the boom times of Las Vegas in the 1950s and early 1960s, the most noteworthy group were, like their higher profile African-American counterparts, also in the entertainment community. Cuban-born band leader Xavier Cugat provided music at the Flamingo. Mexican singing sensation Tito Guizar headlined at the El Rancho Vegas. Latin music, such as the tango from Argentina, caught on in Las Vegas lounges; Brazilian entertainer Carmen Miranda would sing and dance wearing her trademark fruit baskets as hats; and an up-and-coming young bandleader from Cuba named Desiderio Alberto Arnaz y de Acha III charmed audiences with his orchestral magic and cries of "babaloo!" He would later star with wife Lucille Ball on the hit television series I Love Lucy under his more familiar stage name, Desi Arnaz.

For the most part, however, the roles that Hispanics played on Vegas stages during this era were stereotypical and secondary to the big-name acts. They were the jugglers and tumblers, the pianists and back-up bands, the animal-act trainers and chorus-line dancers. A pecking order of sorts developed within the Hispanic community, with Latinos from South America and of Spanish descent in higher positions than their Puerto Rican and Chicano brethren.

Like the city's African Americans, most Las Vegas Hispanics in the 1950s lived "across the tracks" on the Westside or else north of the city limits, where real estate was available, taxes were low, and dilapidated housing was cheap, although often lacking in access to electricity, running water, and sewerage. Many Las Vegans saw these ghettos as an embarrassment, but at least one city father, new Las Vegas Mayor Oran K. Gragson, realized they were also an opportunity.

Gragson, a former Texan, had come to Las Vegas in the 1930s to work on Boulder Dam. He later managed the Boulder Inn and owned a second-hand store, then a furniture store, with his wife Bonnie. His tenure from 1959 until 1975 would make him the longest serving mayor in Las Vegas history, a period in which he would institute a streets and highway commission (later the Regional Transportation Commission), attract a $1.6-million Manpower anti-poverty program from Washington, and add parks and recreational facilities that serve the community even today. By the early 1960s, Gragson had already shown his penchant for reform by ridding the city's police ranks of a burglary ring and forcing the tainted chief of police and a corrupt city manager to resign their posts.

In 1964, a Hispanic and African-American suburb called Vegas Heights was annexed north of the city by the metropolitan government. This minority neighborhood was composed of trailers and ramshackle houses, but rather than raze the area for urban development, Gragson and his City Planning Office were determined to raise funds for improvements that would pave streets, modernize sewage and electrical systems, and otherwise bring the decaying suburban homes and businesses up to code. The district soon became cleaner and safer. Property values improved. Hispanics began returning to the community; by the 1970 census, they would number 3,871 in Las Vegas proper and nearly 10,000 in the metropolitan area.

At the same time, Gragson brought relief to the Las Vegas Colony of Southern Paiute. The Native American tribe had not received much support from any government agency in the turbulent 1950s. The Bureau of Indian Affairs and the Clark County Council of Social Agencies wanted the colony's residents to sell their land and relocate. Official records were "lost" and funding applications were denied or tabled. Authorities began claiming, "this group is not an identifiable tribe or band," so the Paiute were not really entitled to the land reserved for "tribal use." Even as the bickering intensified, man-made wells dug on colony property began to collapse and dry up. One of the main wells was condemned and water had to be hauled to the reservation from other sources.

In 1961, Mayor Gragson stepped in and convinced federal officials that it was in everyone's best interests to improve the land, rather than force its sale. City water and sewerage services were extended to the colony in 1962. The tribe would have to continue to fight, alongside other minorities, for full rights and reparations for several years to come, but at least the first steps in recognition of their plight and sovereignty had been taken.

Water, of course, was everyone's concern. In the same year the Paiute got their city source, the old Las Vegas Springs dried up. Life in the region was now almost totally dependent on the resources of Lake Mead. As huge as the reservoir was, its waters were not readily available to valley residents. California had laid excessive claims to the lake's reserves, which were contested by Nevada and Arizona in long drawn-out court battles until settlement could be reached in 1963. The United States Secretary of the Interior was thereafter vested with broad discretion in apportioning water during years of shortage and excess. Anticipating future disputes between the neighboring states and increased demand throughout the Southwest, another huge dam-building Colorado River project was initiated in Glen Canyon along the Arizona–Utah border to create a new regional resource, Lake Powell.

No new hotels were built in the greater Las Vegas area for almost half a dozen years after the 1958 launch of the Stardust. Only slowly did the addition of more rooms and table games come to Fremont Street, with the opening of the Lady Luck in 1964, the Mint in 1965, and the Four Queens in 1966. Over-building on the Strip postponed new resort construction even longer there, with the Aladdin not making its appearance until April 1, 1966. It evolved from an earlier non-casino property, the English Tudor–style Tally Ho, which was briefly renamed the King's Crown. Compared to the existing Strip casinos, the Aladdin was good, but not spectacular. Apart from some fine restaurants and a nine-hole golf course inherited from the former property owners, the new resort's main claim to fame was the wedding of Priscilla Beaulieu to Elvis Presley there on May 1, 1967.

What Las Vegas needed to get people excited again was the opening of something truly extravagant, palatial, historic, and beyond the imagination of any previous developer. That is exactly what Jay Sarno, a man of far-sighted vision, had in mind.

Backed by money from the Teamster's pension fund and the friendship of union boss Jimmy Hoffa, Sarno had developed Cabana motor lodges across the country, from California to Georgia. His idea for Las Vegas was to recreate a kingdom of fantasy and pleasure that would be "fit for an emperor." His resort would be the first truly themed hotel in Las Vegas—Caesars Palace—with 34 acres of expansive gardens, marble statues, glistening fountains, pillared entrances, 680 plush guest rooms, and a 14-story tower.

Constructed at a cost of $24 million, Caesars Palace was a hit from the very start. The 1,800 guests who attended the million-dollar August 5, 1966 grand opening were spoiled with filet mignon, caviar, and the finest champagne. For three full days, toga-clad cocktail waitresses wearing Greco-Roman pony-tailed wigs would "slave" for the occasion's Caesars and Cleopatras. Each night, the invitees were treated to opening acts by Andy Williams and the Lennon Sisters in an 800-seat theater, Circus Maximus. In years to follow, it would showcase almost all of the major names in show business: Diana Ross, Tony Bennett, George Burns, Cher, Paul Anka, Milton Berle, Tom Jones, Julio Iglesias, Willie Nelson, and of course Sinatra.

What made Caesars special, however, was not its extravagant fixtures, top entertainers, or fine food. Sarno had based the resort on a totally new premise that pervaded every aspect of it—that people came to Las Vegas not only to gamble but to play. They wanted to escape their everyday lives and lose themselves in a world of fantasy. They dreamed of living like emperors and empresses, and Caesars could turn those dreams into reality, if only for the length of a short vacation.

Two years later, on October 16, 1968, Sarno proved his point by opening yet another land of fantasy on the Strip nearby—Circus Circus—a place of clowns, trapeze artists, jugglers, dancing bears, game arcades, and fun for the whole family. It had no hotel at first, just a casino, restaurants, and a showroom. But it worked because "everyone loves to go to the circus."

Jay Sarno did not invent Las Vegas, but he had discovered its secret power—the one that had attracted to the desert valley Brigham Young, William Andrews Clark, Tony Cornero, Benjamin Siegel, and so many other visionaries before him. Knowledge of that secret would soon be shared by a new generation of big dreamers, one of whom would wrest control of the city and the Strip away from the Syndicate and brand Las Vegas with his own unique character—Howard Robard Hughes Jr.

Chapter Six

ENTER THE MILLIONAIRES

Howard Hughes arrived in Las Vegas quietly by train in the dark, pre-dawn hours of November 27, 1966. His aides whisked him by car to the Desert Inn where they had reserved the top two floors for the enigmatic tycoon and his entourage. Hughes needed privacy, not the raucous gaiety of the casino crowd. Unlike his previous visits to the Strip, he had come not to play but to stay.

Born on Christmas Eve 1905, Hughes was only 18 when he dropped out of college to take over an inherited business. His father had died in 1924, leaving behind a tool manufacturing company that held the patent rights to a drilling bit used by oil companies, not only in Hughes's home state of Texas, but throughout the world. Over the next four decades, the young heir would turn the family fortune into a billion-dollar empire, successfully launching into Hollywood filmmaking, aircraft development, and commercial air services. His movie studios discovered Paul Muni, Jean Harlow, and Jane Russell. Hughes gained fame for himself as a test pilot, soloing around the world in 1938 and surviving a near-fatal crash in an experimental photo reconnaissance plane near Beverly Hills eight years later. His stake in Trans World Airlines (TWA) would be worth $584 million by May 1966, when he sold the company and started his journey on a spending spree America had never seen before, nor was likely to see ever again.

Such staggering wealth required that Hughes seek a more hospitable tax haven than his home in southern California, where he often felt like "a small fish in the big pond." The Bahamas, the Mediterranean, and England were considered, but Hughes preferred an American domicile. At the same time, his financial advisors, many of them Mormons who knew banker Parry Thomas, had explained how the passive income he would receive from his TWA windfall would be taxed at a higher rate than active income earned from investments, such as casino ownership. And what better place was there to own casinos in the 1960s than the city that glowed neon-bright in the southern Nevada desert?

It was an easy decision. Hughes had long had a love for Las Vegas. Since the 1940s, he had often frequented the El Rancho and the Last Frontier. He was said to be a terrible gambler, who lost his temper when losing, but he enjoyed the lifestyle, the 24-hour atmosphere, and most probably the showgirls as well. Hughes had cultivated a lifestyle in Hollywood. He was an incurable womanizer, divorced from Houston socialite Ella Rice and estranged from his second wife, actress Jean Peters. The playboy could easily see himself living in a city without clocks where morals were loose. What's more, he could get the respect that he craved. "I want people to pay attention when I talk," he had declared. In Las Vegas, where money talked, people would listen.

Moe Dalitz, the Syndicate's owner of the Desert Inn, had been informed that Hughes and company would be staying for ten days. Christmas and New Year's were coming up and Dalitz needed the best floors to accommodate high rollers. When the group failed to check out, Hughes's representative was told that they had to leave or else they would be kicked out. A call from the Teamster's Jimmy Hoffa convinced Dalitz to let them stay through the holidays, but when Hughes was still there in January, it looked like time to make good on the threat. "If you want a place to sleep," an aide told Hughes, "you'd damned well better buy the hotel." So that's exactly what Hughes did, after a bit of haggling, for $13.25 million.

This signaled the beginning of one of the biggest buying binges ever undertaken by an individual in Las Vegas. After the purchase of the Desert Inn, Hughes asked his Nevada consultant, Robert Maheu, "How many more of these toys are available?" Many more, indeed, were available, and at a time when some of the mob owners were apparently ready to relinquish their power and holdings.

Back when the Kefauver crime committee investigated ownership of casinos in the early 1950s, the Italian Mafia owned next to nothing in town. Meyer Lansky's Syndicate—a confederation of Jewish, Irish, Italian, Polish, and other mobsters—had taken the lead, muscling the old California gamblers aside. During the booming late 1950s, however, the Mafia had slowly gained shares in the Sands, the Riviera, the Sahara, and other hotel-casinos. The two powerful forces declared the valley a free trade zone, where neither would lose and both could profit. Ownership of properties changed hands many times. Silent partners were everywhere.

Within the gang-owned casinos, "skimming" had increased year by year as managers pocketed uncounted revenues, which would be used to finance illegal activities elsewhere in the country. Skimming was part of business, but theft was not. Anyone found guilty of stealing from them was sent for a cleansing "sand bath" in the desert from which no one ever returned. But the criminal element had grown so large, they could no longer police themselves effectively. Renegade Mafioso began freelancing in illegal drugs and prostitution. The streets were no longer as safe as they had been in the 1950s.

Moreover, since 1959, a five-man State Gaming Commission had begun cracking down on license infringements and was seeking to rid the casinos of mob ownership. Tax revenues from gambling paid for welfare and education, as well as other government programs. Such functions could not be funded by "dirty money." The state's goal was to make sure the casino owners were "so clean they squeaked." Into the commissioners' hands fell a report on "Mafia-controlled properties" based upon a study ordered by Attorney General Robert F. Kennedy in the early 1960s. The heat was on in Las Vegas and getting more intense. Feeling it, many of the boys were happy to take a quick profit by selling out to a high bidder.

In short order, Hughes bought the $14.6-million Sands, the $3-million Castaways, and the $14-million (Last) Frontier, just months after it received major renovation and a new name in 1967. Many of these investment decisions were influenced by Hughes's Mormon confidants, whom he trusted and relied on more than any other advisors. Over the next four years, no fewer than five Mormon "secretary-nurses" attended to Hughes—Howard Eckersley, Roy Crawford, John Holmes, Lavar Myler, and George Francom. LDS executives in Los Angeles directed the cadre.

A surprising purchase—not recommended by the Mormon contingent—was that of the Silver Slipper. It was a tiny casino next to the Frontier, which drew attention to itself by displaying a much larger than life, bejeweled and sparkling, high-heeled slipper that rotated around and around in front of the building. It seems that the toe of the slipper would stop its revolution for a few moments, and then begin again, pointing at the Desert Inn and the windows of the suite occupied by Hughes. Even though the windows had black-out curtains, the revolution of the slipper was quite apparent to the annoyed guest. He also believed there were probably cameras inside the toe, which took pictures of him in his suite each time it stopped. Instead of arguing with the management of the Silver Slipper, he did what he often did in times such as these: he bought the place. After that, the slipper only turned on his say-so and did not make its periodic stops, pointing its toe at him.

Hughes's sixth casino purchase was the half-finished Landmark, begun in 1964 by Frank Carroll of Kansas City, which was a true landmark in appearance. Its space-age circular restaurant floors crowned a 31-story tower modeled after Seattle's Space Needle and its unusually designed rooms, each pie-sliced, surrounded the central bank of elevators. Opened on July 1, 1969 at a cost of $20 million, it was located to the east of Highway 91, making it the first off-Strip major hotel-casino in Las Vegas history.

Oddly enough, corporations were not really allowed to own casinos in Nevada at that time. The Gaming Commission could not investigate the background of every shareholder in a major business, so they excluded holdings by commercial firms and limited ownership to individuals they could check. In 1961, Del Webb Corporation—whose head, Delbert Eugene Webb, was a close personal friend of Hughes, as well as Bugsy Siegel's contractor for the construction of the original Flamingo—had managed to get around the rule, buying and owning the Sahara as a hotel and having a properly licensed tenant (Consolidated Casinos, Inc.) run the gaming operations. The tenant paid rent (gambling profits) to the landlords (Webb's associates Milton Prell, L.C. Jacobson, and Alfred Winter). In similar fashion, Webb acquired the old Thunderbird on the Strip and the Mint downtown. The fact that the landlords and the tenant were actually the same people did not seem to bother the state authorities, as long as they were sure everyone was squeaky clean. The backing of Mormon banker Parry Thomas in Webb's projects simply added to the arrangements' respectability.

In Hughes's case, he was the sole owner of Hughes Tool Company, so no extensive background check of shareholders was necessary. No one can recall the billionaire ever appearing before the Gaming Commission to apply for a license, but his "good name and reputation" seemed sufficient. His obvious wealth did not hurt his cause either.

Hughes had also wanted to buy the Stardust for $30.5 million, which would have given his group of gaming properties control over one-seventh of Nevada's entire gross gambling revenues. State officials were not opposed to the purchase. They saw Hughes as cleaning out mob interests and legitimizing gambling as a real business. Authorities in Washington, however, did not agree. President Lyndon Baines Johnson's Department of Justice and the Securities and Exchange Commission came down hard on the deal, invoking anti-trust laws to block the Stardust's sale. No more Nevada casinos for the reclusive billionaire.

If Hughes couldn't buy any more gambling operations, then there were other ways to spend his money in Las Vegas. In short order, he purchased a restaurant, a motel, a small airline, an airport, gold and silver mines scattered across the state, tracts of valuable undeveloped land along the Las Vegas Strip, 100-odd residential lots, and a $3.5-million television station. Then he came up with a scheme to buy out all of the race and sports books in town—a page from Meyer Lansky's original plan for the city—and establish a worldwide bookmaking operation where people could contact his company in Las Vegas and bet on literally anything they wanted to. That particular project fell through, but it gives an apt notion of the scale of his thinking.

Because Hughes did not himself keep a close watch over his accounts, entrusting such work to his aides and advisors, he was susceptible to "skimming" by his own staff and casino managers. A report later issued by the IRS indicated as much as $50 million was siphoned from the profits of his holdings by 1970. No matter who was responsible, it happened on Robert Maheu's watch. Hughes sacked his key advisor, leaving his trusted Mormon staff virtually in full charge of his holdings, including casino operations. Sinful or not, the Latter Day Saints were connected to gambling.

Hughes's time in Las Vegas changed not only the city, but also the man. Even as his power, wealth, and reputation grew, he drew more inward, more suspicious of threats to his enterprises and his health. He hid from the public eye and would see only a handful of close friends and advisors. Even phone conversations were avoided. His dependence on drugs steadily increased and his paranoia deepened. What finally drove Hughes out of Las Vegas was the federal government's plans for an increase in atomic bomb detonations (which had gone underground, by this point) less than 100 miles from Las Vegas. This terrified the billionaire, compounding all the other issues that bothered him and hastening his decline into mental illness. Sometime between November 5 and Thanksgiving Day, 1970, almost exactly four years after his arrival, Hughes and his band of close advisors made a mysterious exodus from Las Vegas. Even the local news was unaware of his early morning departure on a stretcher, delivered to Nellis Air Force Base, from where he was flown away to the Bahamas.

Hughes died in April 1976, reportedly of kidney failure. The Summa Corporation, his holding company, took charge of his Las Vegas operations. Hughes's impact on the city was long-lasting and dramatic, still evident today not only in corporate holdings, but also the beautifully landscaped business and residential area that bears his name along Howard Hughes Parkway east of the Strip. When he arrived, Las Vegas was still mainly mob-owned. When he left, it had become a corporate town—a newly opened playground for millionaires.

Unlike Howard Hughes, Kirk Kerkorian was not born into wealth, but like Hughes, he became a billionaire and changed the face of Las Vegas. Born to an Armenian turkey farmer in 1917, he held many jobs growing up and he learned early some excellent business and horse-trading skills: buying something at a low cost, timing being everything, and then selling at a huge profit. His interest in flying and airlines led him to become a major shareholder in Transinternational Airlines and then Western Airlines.

In Las Vegas, Kerkorian bought the property on which Caesars Palace now sits and leased it to Jay Sarno for four years, making a huge profit. He then sold the property for $5 million. In 1967, he purchased land just east of the Strip, on Paradise Road, and began building the largest hotel casino in Las Vegas at the time, named the International. He raced against Hughes to finish the project before Hughes could complete the Landmark, but lost by just a day, opening on July 2, 1969. Among the hotel-casino's noteworthy headliners were Barbra Streisand and an entertainer who had failed in his first attempt to please Las Vegas audiences in the mid-1950s: Elvis Presley. Even as construction was going on, Kerkorian bought the old Flamingo and made it a "hotel school" for the employees of the future International. He would sell both the properties to Hilton Hotels, Inc. within a year of obtaining ownership—at a profit, as always.

In 1971, Kerkorian was off shopping in Hollywood, where he purchased Metro-Goldwyn-Mayer (MGM) Studios. He would use many of its props and copyrights in his plans for his next big venture, the original MGM Grand Hotel and Casino (now Bally's), completed on December 5, 1973 at a cost of over $100 million. It was built on the site of the Bonanza, a small hotel-casino attempt by lawyer Larry Wolf and his wife in 1967, meant to recapture the old frontier theme that had all but disappeared from Las Vegas by then. Kerkorian had snapped up the property when the revival attempt failed. By contrast, with 2,100 rooms, a 1,200-seat showroom, and 4,500 employees, the new hotel-casino was the largest resort in the world.

The MGM Grand was right out of classic Hollywood, with the movie *Grand Hotel* as inspiration for its name. Scenes from *Gone with the Wind*, *Singing in the Rain*, and other hits were drawn into its design. Hotel hallways were lined with large black and white glossy photos of the reigning stars of the MGM Golden Era, such as Elizabeth Taylor, Clark Gable, and Judy Garland. The restaurants were all named after famous movies or actors: Barrymores and Gigi's. Everything was done in first-class elegance. Besides the gigantic stadium-sized casino, there was a huge shopping area, swimming, tennis, jai alai, and even a classic movie theatre, where guests could sit in easy-chair comfort, with drinks served by waitresses. It seems that every time one of his hotels was up and running, Kerkorian would routinely sell it to someone and start building another, making huge profits each time. This one, however, was a true gem and he would hold on to it for a decade.

"The times they are a-changin' "—the lyrics of a 1964 Bob Dylan song—described the social backdrop against which Hughes and Kerkorian made their commercial buy-outs of the mob. It was the Age of Aquarius—a shift from the black and white days of the 1950s to a day-glow-colored era of new consciousness. Love and peace were "in;" fighting and war were not. America had become embroiled in a bloody conflict in distant Vietnam, the Protest Movement challenged the status quo, and the cry for civil rights was being heard across the nation.

In Las Vegas, the closure of the Moulin Rouge had galvanized the will of African Americans on the Westside. They demanded the right to visit and stay in the segregated hotel-casinos of Las Vegas and hold jobs heretofore restricted to whites. In March 1960, Las Vegas NAACP President Dr. James B. McMillan, a local dentist, warned Mayor Oran Gragson that there would be organized protests in the city if he did not come up with a plan to eliminate racial discrimination. Fearful of the harm such demonstrations could cause to convention business and the tourist trade, and under the urging of liberal mediators like *Las Vegas Sun* founder Hank Greenspun, city officials and casino owners gathered with the protesters and reluctantly agreed to establish new policies, narrowly averting a declared March 26 civil rights march down Las Vegas Boulevard. Because this meeting was held in the Westside's closed hotel-casino, the resulting accord was called The Moulin Rouge Agreement—a crucial first step in what would be a turbulent decade of movement to integrate the area's races.

Not long after, however, reports of continued discrimination started circulating. Sympathetic to the cause, Governor Grant Sawyer introduced new state legislation against employment segregation and established the Nevada Equal Rights Commission in 1961. The following year, the commission learned that Las Vegas hotel-casino operators were still hiring very few if any non-Caucasians. Only "a scattering of Orientals" had been given positions. Their excuse: a lack of "qualified" non-white applicants for positions as bartenders, waiters, waitresses, and office personnel. The color barriers were still very much in place and the state commission had no power to do anything about it. Activists had proposed bringing civil rights authority under the Gaming Control Commission's wing, but political interests wanted gambling control kept separate.

Enter the Millionaires

Over the next two years, Las Vegas minorities, led by the NAACP, called for desegregation of public housing and schools. Nationwide civil rights legislation passed by Congress in 1964 prompted the Nevada state legislature to tighten its laws, resulting in the March 30, 1965 passage of A.B. 404, a bill that outlawed discrimination on the basis of creed, color, or race in public accommodations and employment in places where workers numbered 15 or more. Another victory had been won, but the celebrations were brief. Many casinos downtown and on the Strip defied the new regulations. Public places had been opened to people of all races, but discrimination still persisted in housing and employment. Primary schools were still segregated, too. Protests were held, which turned from peaceful to militant in 1967 and 1968. Then, in January 1969, the situation escalated to violence as fighting broke out among local teenagers, leading to intervention by riot-gear-clad North Las Vegas police at Rancho High. Days later, an African-American student at Las Vegas High School was thrown through a trophy case during a racial fracas. And then a sit-in meeting by black students at Clark High School triggered a wild melee by over 1,000 rioters, prompting officials to temporarily close the school and lock down others. On February 3, the schools reopened, all but Las Vegas High, with police guards on hand.

For a while, order was restored, but again the peace was short-lived. In the Westside on October 6, 23 persons ended up in the hospital as local gangs went on a rampage and 200 Las Vegas police officers were called in to bring order to the streets. A curfew was enforced on the area, but in the weeks ahead, incidents of rock throwing occurred and fires broke out, tear gas was used, and arrests mounted. The unrest continued in spurts and waves into the next year.

Not until 1971 did firm and enforceable laws came into effect, defusing the explosive racial tension and opening the way to true integration of Las Vegas communities. A consent decree was signed by local hotels and unions, pledging an end to discriminatory employment practices. This time, they meant it. Unpopular though it was among many white parents, bussing orders forced the desegregation of the valley's elementary schools. Children of all races would grow up studying and playing together. New state legislation assured open housing and Westside residents gradually began to move into other area neighborhoods.

The painful shift to racial equality and integration was led primarily by local African Americans, but the Chicano Movement played a role, too. In 1960, only 578 Hispanics lived in the Las Vegas area. The number would swell to 9,937 by 1970 and 34,998 by 1980, compared with a growth from 11,005 to 24,760 to 46,064 for the African-American population in the same decades. Chicanos and other Latinos were drawn to the city by increasing job opportunities, but their living standards remained poor. Although technically Caucasian, for the best-paying work they were not considered "white enough." In 1968, the Nevada Association of Latin Americans (NALA) was established in Las Vegas to work along with the NAACP to institute change. In 1971 and 1972, Chicano students at the University of Nevada, Las Vegas (UNLV) formed an activist group called La Raza Student Organization and pressured the administration to implement a Chicano studies program and hire Chicano faculty. Their petitions prompted the hiring of at least two such lecturers and the launch of ethnic studies classes within the field of social anthropology. It was about this time that the term Hispanic came into vogue, bringing together Americans of Mexican, Puerto Rican, Cuban, and other Latino origins under a single integrating concept. Not everyone liked being lumped together with peoples who often disagreed, but the new grouping gave them a political base more powerful than Chicanos alone could claim and a way to bond together on issues of common concern, such as housing, jobs, and education.

At the same time, members of the Las Vegas Colony of Southern Paiute fought to be compensated for the lands taken from them over the years. Nothing could restore the tribal culture and heritage that had been destroyed, but they deserved the right to self-determination. Their civil rights had been violated as clearly as anyone's. In agreement, the government's Indian Claims Commission awarded the Las Vegas Paiute $8.25 million in reparations in 1968. Bureau of Indian Affairs officials once again tried to convince the tribe to sell their land and move, to use the money to relocate. But by now the colony governed its own affairs. A new constitution and bylaws were drawn up by the tribe and approved by the United States Secretary of the Interior on July 22, 1970. Soon after, Kenneth Anderson was installed as the colony's chairman, a post he would hold for many years after. Defining tribal membership became an important issue, as did housing and road access. More land was needed. Economic alternatives had to be studied in order to use the new funds wisely. These matters would preoccupy the tribe through the remainder of the decade.

Even though the various civil rights organizations of the 1960s and 1970s were not always unified in their goals or in agreement over courses of action, their efforts changed the complexion of the Las Vegas Valley into a true melting pot of cultures and races. Pacific Islanders, East Indians, Vietnamese, Laotians, Filipinos, and other Asian immigrants began to arrive in the valley during the 1970s. The fight for equality benefited white minorities, too, such as Italian Americans—who were certainly not all mobsters and had suffered their own forms of ethnic discrimination earlier in the century—and people of the Jewish and Mormon faiths—not all millionaires by any means—who were often shunned by followers of other religions. As Howard Hughes and Kirk Kerkorian shaped the face of Las Vegas with financial wealth, so did 1960s activists who invested their wealth of spirit in the community, including James McMillan and Kenneth Anderson, and Lubertha Johnson before them.

Even more than in past decades, Las Vegas became "all about image" in this period of social change. And when it came to projecting the city's character, no one had done it better than its famous millionaires of talent, the Rat Pack. With the mob on the run, Las Vegas needed to shake off its wild, lawless persona and present a clean new entertainment face to the world. What stars could possibly be bright enough to eclipse the Sinatra–Davis–Martin bad-boy image?

One of the first was a Polish-Italian stage artist, just four years Sinatra's junior, who had debuted at the Last Frontier two years before the Chairman of the Rat Pack had presided over his first Helldorado parade—Wladziu Valentino "Walter" Liberace. If glitter, glamour, and opulence were what the new Las Vegas was all about, no one exemplified it better than the rhinestone- and sequin-bedecked master pianist known as Mister Showmanship.

Liberace had originally come to Las Vegas at the invitation of Maxine Lewis, entertainment director of the Last Frontier. In 1944, his salary was $750 a week. Combining classical tunes with boogie-woogie, smiles, and friendly small talk, he developed a style unique even in a city filled with talent. Before long, he had a ten-year contract with the hotel and his salary doubled. During that time, he had an embarrassing encounter with a tall, disheveled man whom he thought was a lighting engineer. It happened to be Howard Hughes, who had come backstage from a visit to the casino for a look-see. Liberace also had a run-in, in 1947, with "Bugsy" Siegel, who wanted to steal him for shows at the Flamingo. Afraid to refuse, yet unwilling to work for the mob, Liberace was saved from making a decision by Siegel's assassination.

Central to Liberace's popularity were his fancy-beyond-words costumes, his rhinestone-studded pianos, his incredibly-gifted talent, and his boyish charm, brightness, and exuberance on stage. He moved on to other venues in town, including the Riviera in 1953, where he was paid $50,000 a week. Ostrich feathers, exotic furs, bugle beads, and jeweled rings were just a few of the many items in his extravagant wardrobe. An ornate silver candelabra became his trademark. Classic cars became a passion. But Liberace's image was not about riches as much as it was richness, a quality he managed to convey to fans not only in live performances, but also on television, where he was given a nationwide audience. He symbolized what *Time* magazine would call "glorious excess."

Accepting in 1972 a salary offer of $300,000 per week, more than any Las Vegas entertainer had ever earned, Liberace opened at the Las Vegas Hilton and made the city his legal residence. The mansion he created as his home was decorated in pure Liberace style, with an indoor lagoon, finishes of gold, marble, and mirror, and even a reproduction of Michelangelo's Sistine Chapel ceiling painting above his bed. To hold the overflow of treasures he collected, the virtuoso of pageantry built a museum on East Tropicana Avenue, inaugurated on Easter Sunday 1979. It would become a popular tourist attraction and remain so, long after his final Las Vegas performance on the stage of Caesars Palace in 1986. He died the following year at age 67.

Even as Mister Showmanship was becoming Mister Las Vegas, another performer was getting ready to don Sinatra's crown. This singer had briefly shared the stage with

Liberace at the Last Frontier in the 1950s and he returned in 1969 to claim a spotlight of his own—Elvis Presley.

The once-and-future "King" seemed to be nearing the end of his career before his opening at Kirk Kerkorian's new International Hotel. Presley had bombed in Las Vegas in 1956, at that time too much a teen idol to wow the older casino crowd. His plotless off-the-rack movies of the 1960s were mainly showcases for his songs, which had a hard time selling against the Beatles, the Supremes, and other musicians of the day. Only his silver screen chemistry with dancer-actress Ann-Margaret in the starring roles of *Viva Las Vegas* gave Presley a tie to the city. To Las Vegas, he was a tourist, who would sometimes bring his entourage in a huge tour bus from Los Angeles to the desert for fun and games. The "pelvis" that had shocked and delighted an earlier generation now seemed anachronistic. Could he follow in Sinatra's footsteps and make Las Vegas his comeback town?

People had forgotten how charismatic Presley could be in person. For his appearance at the International, he had gotten himself into shape with martial arts exercise. He wore his now-famous karate-style white jumpsuit covered in sequins, à la Liberace. The King was back and better than ever! The International experienced an onslaught of hysterical fan club members, 100 percent room occupancy, sold-out showrooms nightly, and the attendant attraction of other name performers in the lounges, such as B.B. King. When Presley was around, there was an electricity that filled the whole resort, never to be matched again.

Realizing a great thing when they saw and heard it, the International's management offered the returning star a five-year contract, paying him $125,000 a week for eight weeks of shows a year. Before Presley's comeback, many say the city was losing its grip on the title of Entertainment Capital of the World. Gambling had become too much the focus. In a way, the return of the King was a resurrection for the Kingdom. As Caesars Palace creator Jay Sarno had surmised, people came to Las Vegas to lose themselves in the fantasy—to play. The broad appeal of a reinvented Elvis Presley helped refocus attention on the showrooms. Although hit acts like the Beatles had passed through before, contemporary performers had begun to think of Las Vegas as the last stop in a career. Presley made them begin to see other possibilities. Perhaps careers could be started and restarted here, too.

Next to Graceland, Las Vegas would become the location most identified with Presley. In return, the King would live on—long after his tragic 1977 death by drug overdose—in the city's evergreen Elvis impersonators, Elvis museums, and Elvis-branded memorabilia.

The old ways died slowly, but they were most definitely on the way out by the 1970s. MBAs replaced street smarts as the desired credentials for managers and the new corporate hotel-casino structures began to evaluate operations differently. Accountability, bottom lines, return on investment, risk management . . . these were the words that replaced friends, favors, and fate as the determining factors in decision-making. Food and beverage services, entertainment, rooms, and gaming became separate profit centers. The free shows and junkets of the past were no longer seen as cost-efficient means of drawing in gamblers and their money. Stars such as Robert Goulet, who commanded $65,000 a week in the early 1970s, discovered themselves overpriced. Many entertainers were simply overexposed, "the same headliners all the time," and incapable of drawing paying crowds. New attractions were needed.

The 1960s had seen several shifts in the focus of Las Vegas entertainment, not the least of which was a heightened interest in sports. From its very first championship boxing match, with Benny "Kid" Paret claiming the welterweight title over Don Jordan in a bout hosted by the Las Vegas Convention Center in 1960, to the launch of the city's first major tennis tournament—The Howard Hughes Open Tennis Championship—at the Frontier in 1969, Las Vegas embraced competitive events one after another. Horseracing flourished briefly (1963–1965) on a three-eighths-mile oval track owned by the Thunderbird. And in 1969, Mint owner Del Webb decided to bring a new kind of action to Las Vegas—off-road racing. He inaugurated the Mint 400 in the rugged desert terrain outside town and it quickly became one of the area's top sporting events.

In the years that followed, virtually every sport under the sun (and all of those played under roofs), would be tried and tested as allures for tourism. These included the "fastest sport in the world"—the Spanish ball and basket game called jai alai—played at the MGM Grand in 1973, championship ice skating at the Flamingo Hilton in 1982, the debut of professional baseball (an exhibition game between the Padres and the Mariners) to inaugurate Cashman Field, the launch of the Panasonic Las Vegas Invitational golf tournament in 1983, and the relocation of the National Finals Rodeo to the city in 1985. But of all the sports introduced to Las Vegas, the one that packed the most punch was boxing. The most famous names in the ring would be brought to the city by its passionate crowds, world-class facilities, and huge purses; among them, one man would stand out as the champion among champions—Muhammad Ali.

Fighting under his birth name, Cassius Marcellus Clay Jr., Ali had become the world's heavyweight boxing king by defeating Sonny Liston in 1964. His first official title defense came in 1965, when he faced former champion Floyd Patterson at the Las Vegas Convention Center. It was a thrilling bout, which Ali won convincingly by technical knockout in the 12th round, proving to disbelievers that he was, indeed, "The Greatest" among all fighters in the ring.

Thirteen years later, after losing and regaining the heavyweight crown, Ali would lose it once again in a split decision taken by relative newcomer Leon Spinks at the Las Vegas Hilton on February 15, 1978. Boxing history followed in September, when Ali took the belt back from Spinks and became the sport's first three-time heavyweight champ.

"The Greatest" retired soon after, but he would come out of retirement and return to Las Vegas one more time, in 1980, for an unprecedented attempt at becoming four-time champion. The fight was held at a million-dollar arena constructed by Caesars Palace especially for the event. Only one obstacle stood in Ali's way and it turned out to be a huge one: world champion Larry Holmes. The undefeated belt-holder stopped the ex-champ in a 15-round decision that proved Holmes's own claim to greatness. Ali would retire permanently the following year, but not before paving the way for generations of great fighters to come—from Sugar Ray Leonard to Oscar De La Hoya—and helping to make Las Vegas the undisputed boxing capital of the world, a title it retains even today.

Millionaires were now making Las Vegas and Las Vegas was making millionaires. One of the latter was just ten years old when he first saw the bright lights of the Strip on a visit with his father, a compulsive gambler, in 1952. His dad taught a lesson by example that he would never forget: the only way to win in a casino was to buy it. Fifteen years later, son Steve Wynn returned on his own with wife Elaine Paschal to buy a little piece of the Frontier Hotel for $45,000 and work there as slot and keno manager. That is exactly when Howard Hughes added the hotel to his shopping cart, which put Wynn out of a job in the ensuing management reshuffle. The young man did a bit of work in lounge show promotions, then obtained a liquor distributorship. That could have been the end of his story, but luckily Wynn had already made his life's most important contact, befriending Parry Thomas of the Bank of Las Vegas.

In 1971, the newcomer discovered a tiny strip of land on Flamingo Road owned by Howard Hughes that was desperately desired by neighboring Caesars Palace. Hughes wouldn't sell to his competitor, which created an opening for a shrewd young entrepreneur. Through Thomas and backed by a loan cosigned by J&B Scotch magnate Abraham Rosenberg, Wynn located and obtained options on a small property the billionaire wanted. A swap and sale was arranged which netted the gambler's son, the Mormon banker, and the whisky maker a cool $1 million.

Wynn next took his share of the profits and began quietly buying into the Golden Nugget, a gaming property owned and operated by laid-back old-timers who had not done much to increase its value over the years. By August 1973, Wynn had purchased enough stock to put himself on the casino's Board and take control. Applying new management techniques, he increased the Golden Nugget's pre-tax profits from $1.1 million to $4.2 million in just a year. He added a hotel tower and, by 1977, the casino's annual turnover was up to $12 million—an incredible figure in the downtown district, which year upon year had been losing business to the Strip properties. He was beating the corporations at their own game.

Wynn built a second Golden Nugget in Atlantic City in 1980. By 1984, his personal net worth was up to an estimated $100 million. Selling the New Jersey property in 1987, Wynn turned his attention back to the Las Vegas Strip, where he envisioned the next breakthrough between fantasy and reality—a new 86-acre resort to be built at a cost of half a billion dollars. It would be named The Mirage.

The opening of this hotel in 1989 was monumental in many ways. Not only was it entrepreneur Steve Wynn's first venture in building a hotel from the ground up in Las Vegas, but it changed the appearance of the strip, as well as bringing a new level of class to the sometimes gaudy and carnival-like atmosphere. Ever since Wynn had dramatically remodeled the Golden Nugget and added hotel towers, he had been looking for a property on Las Vegas Boulevard to add to his collection. He found the property where the Castaways stood, a popular spot that had seen better days. It was in an ideal location, right next to Caesars Palace, and Wynn was able to obtain it from people who were managing Howard Hughes's still substantial property holdings in Las Vegas.

With a tropical island paradise as its theme, the Mirage included rainforest walkways from the main entrance to a huge aquarium located behind the front desk. In front of the property, a massive man-made volcano was constructed to erupt on schedule every night, spewing masses of fire and smoke into the air to the delight of passersby. Another innovation was its opulent and secluded bungalows (each with a private garden and pool) and private residences (apart from the main building), designed specifically for the high rollers and other celebrities, such as Michael Jackson, to enjoy. Also added was a pool for dolphins to swim and be observed by guests and visitors to the resort. Rare white tigers were put in residence under the care and supervision of the Mirage's new headline act, Siegfried and Roy.

Siegfried Fischbacher was born in 1939 and grew up in Rosenheim, Germany. Roy Horn was born in 1944 and grew up in Nordenham, Germany. Siegfried had always been fascinated with magic and Roy had a very special bond with animals. Their paths crossed and their talents combined on an ocean liner, *The Bremen*, in 1959. Siegfried was hired as a magician and Roy, a waiter and busboy, soon became part of the act. Roy suggested that Chico, a cheetah that he had smuggled on board the ship, be incorporated into Siegfried's performance.

Eventually, by way of many other locales, the two landed in Las Vegas in 1970. They both say that from that time on, Las Vegas has basically meant home for them. They first appeared in the Folies Bergere and the Lido de Paris. Then they became a major part of the innovative Hallelujah Hollywood show at the first MGM Grand in 1974. They were partially responsible for bringing family entertainment to Sin City. Their first starring show was "Beyond Belief" at the Frontier in 1982. Five years later, Steve Wynn signed them on to appear in their own-named theater as part of his new wonderland. Their contract was worth a staggering $57 million.

Life in Las Vegas in the 1970s and 1980s was not always peaceful. In mid-1975, the city suffered a massive flash flood that caused more than $1 million in damage and left two dead. One year later, a manmade disaster would cripple hotel-casino operations on the Las Vegas Strip—culinary workers and bartenders walked off their jobs to protest low pay and poor work conditions. The strike lasted three weeks and affected 15 resorts.

Perhaps the worst tragedy of the period, however, was one that could have easily been averted. Journalist Glenn Puit later reported for the *Las Vegas Review-Journal*:

> On the morning of Nov. 21, 1980, the impossible happened at the MGM Grand. Wiring behind a wall in the resort's deli simmered, then burned undetected for hours. The result was a flash fire that spread at a rate of 19 feet per second through the casino. The smoke from this superfire whisked its way through the resort's air-circulation system and trapped victims in hallways, rooms and stairwells.
>
> About 5,000 people were inside the resort when the fire started shortly after 7 a.m. Eighty four of those would die at the scene or in Las Vegas Valley hospitals. Within a year, three more victims would succumb to fire-related injuries. They were largely tourists and MGM employees.
>
> An investigation found the fire seized on the hotel's greed in constructing the resort and on a series of installation and building design flaws. Fire marshals had insisted sprinklers be installed in the casino during the building's construction in 1972. The hotel refused to pay for the $192,000 system, and a Clark County building official sided with the resort. Authorities later said the sprinkler system could have prevented the disaster at the hotel.

The backlash was over $223 million in legal settlements. There was a public—yet not criminal—dressing down of those responsible for enforcing building codes, the resort, and those who built it. Kirk Kerkorian's crown jewel had been indelibly tarnished. So much construction had taken place over the years, it is a wonder such disaster did not occur even sooner, perhaps. The lesson was learned the hard way and Las Vegas would go on to be an undisputed world leader when it came to fire safety.

Las Vegas celebrated its 75th anniversary in 1980. The population of the greater Las Vegas area was approaching the half-million mark (463,087) and representing its cultural diversity, as well as its many marriage services, Sin City could claim more churches per capita than any other city in the United States. Senior citizens from cold regions to the north and east—so-called "snowbirds"—began flocking to Las Vegas to take advantage of the mild winter weather and inexpensive buffets, plentiful accommodations, and top-notch entertainment. McCarran Airport, with its new International Arrivals Building, opened in 1979, unveiled a 20-year, $785-million expansion program to keep pace with tourism growth into the next century. Water from Lake Mead was flowing through the tunnels, pumps, and pipes of the Robert B. Griffith Water Project of the Southern

Nevada Water System, a $76 million network to supply the needs of the Las Vegas Water District, Nellis Air Force Base, Boulder City, Henderson, and North Las Vegas. New hotels and casinos opened one after another as entrepreneurs flocked to the Las Vegas real estate market. The boom times were coming back.

The first new resort added to the Strip in the 1980s was the Imperial Palace, which rose from the Flamingo Capri Motel to the north of the old Flamingo. With its Japanese theme and "love tub" rooms, it was an immediate stand-out among its neighbors. A unique car museum was added on the fifth floor in 1981, displaying some 200 motoring classics—"the world's finest and largest collection of antique, classic, muscle and special interest automobiles." In 1983, a new show opened at the Imperial Palace, "Legends in Concert," which featured impersonators of famous entertainers—John Lennon, Elvis Presley, Marilyn Monroe, and more. It was among the first production shows staged by the casinos—spin-offs of the patented Vegas showgirl acts—which would become increasingly elaborate and singular in nature. "Legends" would win honors as the 1985 Show of the Year and go on to become the longest running independently produced show of its kind in the history of Las Vegas, celebrating 20 continuous years on stage in 2003.

The 1970s had brought the Royal Hotel, the Paddlewheel, the Paradise, Key Largo, Holiday Casino, the Gold Spike, Continental Hotel, Bingo Palace, Maxim, Main Street Station, and the Sundance. Instead of nicknames like Bugsy and Moe, their new owners had suffixes—Inc. and Ltd.—including such chains as Ambassador Inns, Holiday Inn, Hilton Hotels, Park Place Entertainment, Coast Hotels, and Premier Interval Resorts. By 1980, Nevada's five most dominant gaming entities were all publicly traded corporations—Harrah's, Del Webb, the Hilton, Caesars World, and the MGM. Virtually anyone in America could own a piece of the action, just by contacting a stockbroker. Anyone, that is, but a mobster.

In 1979, a key nail had been driven in the coffin of organized crime in Las Vegas when the Gaming Control Board permanently denied an operating license to Frank "Lefty" Rosenthal, chairman of the Argent Corporation, which owned the Stardust. Rosenthal had been installed by San Diego businessman Allen R. Glick in 1974 with a $62.7-million loan from the Teamster's pension fund. Counting room boss Jay Vandermark had been in charge of the skimming; Chicago hood Tony "The Ant" Spilotro had handled enforcement. The Martin Scorcese movie *Casino* would later dramatize the tale of these three holdovers from the 1950s in stark and entertaining detail.

What made the license denial important was the precedent it set. Thereafter, casinos found to have mob connections were treated roughly. The Aladdin was put under a sell or close order when Lebanese underworld affiliate James Tamer and legal counsel Sorkis Webbe continued to operate the casino after license suspension later in the year. When they failed to comply, state agents raided the property, sealed its slot machines, and closed the gaming tables. In 1980, special agent Joseph "Joe" Yablonsky arrived on the scene as the FBI's Las Vegas investigator. He was a 27-year veteran of the bureau and a pioneer in their sting tactics. Fearful of bad publicity, and perhaps also afraid of having their own indiscretions revealed, city officials at first protested this federal interference. However, following a scandal involving corruption at the Tropicana and then several prosecutions, it was clear that the FBI agent was in town to stay until his work was done. Yablonsky soon had the mob on the run. By 1985, Las Vegas casinos would be largely free of their influence.

From the 1970s on, casino investors would simply have to make their millions the new old-fashioned way—combining hard work and big capital with management skill and far-sighted vision. Gaming had become an industry. Competition had become tough. Business opportunities for individuals with tiny bankrolls that could be parlayed into fortunes were disappearing. A few, like Jackie Gaughan and Sam Boyd, were able to create their wealth by slowly building small ownerships into big empires; others, like Bob Stupak, would have to do so by taking bravado and promotional wizardry to stratospheric levels.

Gaughan, Boyd, and Frank Scott had opened the Union Plaza Hotel in 1971 on the site of the old Union Pacific Rail Depot, the very location where the townsite auction was held in 1905. The back of the Union Plaza faced the railroad tracks, where travelers still arrived in Las Vegas, as they had before. The other side of the hotel faced spectacular Fremont Street. In the first year or two, there was a swimming pool on the second floor, just over the porte cochere, which looked out over Glitter Gulch. In 1983, another tower was added and, in 1990, Gaughan bought the property and changed the name simply to the Plaza, especially fitting since, sadly, the trains no longer stopped there anymore.

Jackie Gaughan was born in Nebraska in 1920 and had his first glimpse of Las Vegas when he was stationed at Las Vegas Airbase (now Nellis AFB) during World War II. He eventually settled here with his wife and two sons in 1951. His first involvement with hotels was purchasing an interest in the Boulder Club downtown, then buying into the Flamingo Hotel. Both property owners noticed Gaughan's abilities as a handicapper and sports book operator. In 1961, he opened the Las Vegas Club with two partners. Then he purchased the El Cortez Hotel. It was here that he started offering "fun books," which contained two-for-one dining coupons and vouchers for free rolls of nickels. Gaughan's next purchase was the Western Hotel Casino in 1965; then he built the Union Plaza with partners Scott and Boyd. His philosophy: "Give the customer a good deal and he will come back." Gaughan's son Michael, who studied and practiced law for a time, gave up the legal trade and joined his father full-time in building, buying, and operating successful hotels and casinos. His first venture was the Barbary Coast in 1979, followed later by the Gold Coast, the Orleans, and the Suncoast.

Sam Boyd, who had arrived in Las Vegas by train in 1941 with just $80 in his pocket, had come all the way up through the casino ranks from the bottom. He rose from dealer to pit boss and shift supervisor, to part-owner in the Sahara, then general manager and partner in the Mint Hotel downtown. In 1963, together with his son Bill, Boyd purchased land in the old red-light district, Block 16, and created the California Club, a casino with a southern California beachcombers theme. That launch was followed by the Eldorado Casino in Henderson in 1964 and finally Sam's Town at the intersection of Boulder Highway and Nellis Boulevard. Not much more than a small Western-theme casino and some motel-like rooms when it opened in 1979, Sam's Town eventually evolved into a 13-acre resort complex with 650 rooms, 10,000 square feet of convention space, an enclosed atrium with a water park and animatronic animals, a multiplex cinema, and nightly musical performances. Today, Boyd Gaming Corporation counts 11 casino entertainment properties with operations in Mississippi, Louisiana, and Illinois, as well as Nevada.

Bob Stupak's rise was not as linear as Gaughan's or Boyd's, but equally stellar. Born in Pittsburgh on April 6, 1942, he was Steve Wynn's contemporary. Both men had fathers who were into gambling activities. Like Wynn, Stupak would get to know Parry Thomas and use loan money to build a small fortune. But the Pennsylvanian's speciality was not real estate or finance, it was marketing, learned as a two-for-one coupon book salesman and perfected during a stint in Australia, where he conducted telemarketing operations.

By March 1974, Stupak had arrived in Las Vegas and purchased a 1.5-acre car lot on an underdeveloped portion of Las Vegas Boulevard, the no man's land that separated the city's downtown district from the flashy Strip casinos. There, he erected a slot club, which burned down less than two months later—arson or a faulty air-conditioner the probable causes. He had dreams of something much larger anyway, so with the insurance money and $1 million borrowed from Valley Bank, he constructed a 20-story tower to replace the slot joint. The new casino, named Vegas World, opened in 1979. That day happened to be Friday the 13th and Vegas World's fortunes seemed to start with bad luck and head downhill from there. Location was the main problem. It was too far from both Casino Center and the bustling section of the Strip. Blasting off into promotion mode, Stupak plastered a sign on the building: "The Sky's the Limit." He accepted recklessly high bets, invented statistically enigmatic games ("Crapless Craps," for example), played poker against a computer on national television, and placed a $1-million bet on the outcome of the Super Bowl. The master of hype even unsuccessfully ran for mayor to gain publicity for himself and his venture.

The promotional stunts escalated and to the chagrin of everyone—particularly the Gaming Control Board, which disapproved of such antics—Stupak's huckster tactics worked. By the late 1980s, Vegas World was pulling in over $100 million a year in gaming revenues. Stupak dreamt of creating the world's tallest sign to draw attention to his casino and soon that dream evolved into creating the world's tallest casino—a structure that would define the Las Vegas skyline in much the same way the Sydney Tower dominated its city's profile in Australia—the Stratosphere Tower.

Perhaps the only dream any other Las Vegas builder had on this scale was an earlier project that remained just a dream: Xanadu. It was a magnificent 1,730-room hotel and casino, conceived by Martin Stern, to be backed financially by real estate developer and East Coast casino magnate Donald Trump. Stern was a well-known architect whose signature was seen in the original balconied tower of the Sahara, the design of International Hotel (now the Las Vegas Hilton), and the conical Sands Tower. Stern's Xanadu project was to be located on the southwest corner of Las Vegas Boulevard and Tropicana, where the Excalibur now stands. It had an innovative design, with a massive atrium inside and slanted walls outside. One of its focal points, a very 1970s idea, was a bar suspended high within the atrium that looked like the top part of a long-stemmed champagne glass. Envisioned were cascading "Firefalls," a lush garden fantasy of pergolas and gazebos on the atrium deck overlooking the casino, a huge convention complex, a shopping village called the Bazaar, a multipurpose late-hours discothque. . . . Sadly, the necessary funds never materialized and the project died on the drawing board.

Great fortunes may be easily gained, invested, and lost in Las Vegas, a city that clearly separates winners from losers. Compelling visions, however, have a way of enduring here and elements of Xanadu would survive in the Luxor, Mandalay Bay, the Bellagio, and other mammoth dreamworks of the 1990s. Bob Stupak's landmark tower would also be built. Las Vegas was about to see its skyline and its future take shape.

Chapter Seven

BEYOND THE FIELD OF DREAMS

The final decade of the twentieth century witnessed yet another population doubling in Las Vegas and its surrounding suburbs. In 1990, the greater Las Vegas area counted 715,587 residents. By 2001, the figure would approach 1.4 million. What could account for such phenomenal migration to a desert valley, where the summer temperatures averaged in the 100s, the main industry had no tangible product, and a city had "no reason for being," as some critics argued? Was it avarice? Pleasure-seeking? The attraction of a mirage created by millionaires?

The simplest answer was jobs. In the 1990s, revenues earned from services—rooms, food and beverage, and entertainment—actually surpassed those of gaming. Las Vegas's transition from emphasis on gambling to promotion of tourism, from "fleecing suckers" to satisfying vacationers, became complete. By 2000, more than 125,000 hotel-motel rooms existed in the Las Vegas Valley. A huge array of employees were needed to serve the typical four-day-three-night visitors to those many rooms. Apart from the obvious maids and managers, receptionists and bell staff, tourists needed the services of waiters and waitresses, cooks, bartenders, cleaners, beauticians, store clerks, taxi drivers, pool attendants and lifeguards, masseuses, ticket sellers, singers, comedians, musicians, magicians, and more. Behind the scenes there had to be electricians and plumbers, truck drivers, security guards, telephone operators, landscapers, water and sanitation engineers, and others. To serve the growing community that served the tourists were doctors and dentists, teachers, coaches, librarians, lawyers, bankers and accountants, grocers, pharmacists, firefighters, police officers, clerics, and clerks. Employment opportunities simply snowballed, with the number of local jobs available increasing by nearly 300,000 in the 1990s.

Although Nevada is a "right to work" state and union membership is optional, roughly 30 percent of all workers in the Las Vegas area are card-carrying members of a trade. These include the Nevada Service Employees Union (with about 5,000 members by 2000), the Teamster's (around 4,500), United Food and Commercial Workers Union (3,049), Service Employees International Union (3,032), International Brotherhood of Electrical Workers (1,814), and the Musicians Union (about 1,200 members). Among these many trades, the Culinary Union (with some 50,000 members in 2000) has played a particularly important role in defining the work environment. The group dates back to the New Deal Era in the 1930s and it grew rapidly after World War II. In the mid-1970s and again in the mid-1990s, crippling strikes would pave the way for better employment conditions, not only for culinary workers, but for all employees in the valley. Not only did jobs become plentiful, local labor gained in dignity, accorded the benefits and security that employees seek beyond adequate wages.

Heading into the new millennium, Las Vegas would rank as both the top destination for American tourists and the fastest growing major urban area in the country. An average of 30 million people a year would be descending on Las Vegas after 1995. Many of them—especially young couples looking for a start in life and seniors seeking a place to spend their golden years—would like what they saw and decide to stay. Developers began to find increasing opportunity in the creation of housing, suburban retirement communities in particular. For example, Del Webb Corporation, which had a hand in the construction of many Las Vegas hotel-casinos, made plans to launch a 2,000-home project in February 1996—Sun City MacDonald Ranch—15 miles south of Casino Center. It was followed up in October 1998 by Sun City Anthem in Henderson, which will eventually include 9,300 dwellings.

The opening of spectacular resorts continued in the 1990s, too. In 1993 alone, an incredible 10,422 rooms were added to the fabled Strip. That's over 3.8 million room-nights per year made available. The grand opening of three more mega-resorts, all launched within two months of each other, started on October 15 with a Circus-Circus enterprise, the now-famous Luxor. Named after an ancient Egyptian city popular with tourists, the Luxor was unique in every way. Its central structure was shaped like a pyramid, with a huge atrium (said to be able to hold nine Boeing 747s stacked one on top of one another), including 2,526 rooms inside. From its apex, rising 350 feet into the sky, beamed a 40-billion-candlepower xenon beam of light—the world's brightest—seen by pilots 250 miles away in Los Angeles and allegedly visible as far as the moon. The Luxor's night light would guide people across the desert like a beacon toward Las Vegas.

Close on the heels of the Luxor's debut, only 12 days later, the Treasure Island opened with 2,891 rooms. This was Steve Wynn's second endeavor on the Strip, following the success of his Mirage four years earlier. Not satisfied with "just another Las Vegas hotel opening," Wynn orchestrated it to be part of the spectacular implosion of another long-standing icon of the Strip, the Dunes, which he planned to replace with the Bellagio. Treasure Island's *Buccaneer Bay* had its first spectacular pirate show, a free performance, which gained a new, sexy twist to the swashbuckling action, "The Sirens of T.I.," in October 2003.

Weeks later, the third major property joined the Strip. On December 18, 1993, the new MGM Grand Hotel and Casino opened, with a staggering 5,005 rooms, making it the largest hotel in the United States, surpassing the medieval-themed Excalibur just across the Tropicana intersection, which had opened in 1990 with 4,032 rooms. Kirk Kerkorian was the owner of the new property. His latest project took the original concept of the MGM Grand and expanded it. Its emerald green buildings were designed with the theme of the *Wizard of Oz* in mind. The original entrance had visitors walking through the mouth of a huge lion and encountering the city of Oz, replete with a flying witch in the sky and an opportunity to walk down the yellow brick road with Dorothy and other Oz characters. There were three additional themes in the original casino: Monte Carlo, Hollywood, and Sports. The hotel-casino occupied an enormous 171,500 square feet—bigger than New York's Yankee Stadium. Its grounds consisted of 112 acres, offering plenty of room for expansion. With the addition of the New York-New York hotel-casino to the busy Tropicana intersection in 1997, the "Four Corners" properties (MGM, Tropicana, Excalibur, and NYNY) would by themselves hold more hotel rooms than the entire city of San Francisco.

An adjunct of the huge MGM hotel was its 16,325-seat Grand Garden Arena, which was inaugurated by Barbra Streisand on December 31, 1993. The arena has since been used for everything from professional ice-skating shows to wrestling events, major prize fights, rodeos, and super-star concerts. The 33-acre MGM Grand Adventures Theme Park was another first in Las Vegas. Envisioned as a smaller version of Anaheim's popular Disneyland, it was a self-contained theme park, which took the level of attractions for kids and families in Las Vegas up several notches. Other hotels, such as Circus-Circus, Excalibur, and the Luxor, had whole floors that offered arcades and games, but Grand Adventures had all that, plus live entertainment and thrill rides.

Las Vegas in the 1990s was attempting to shed its "adults only" image and appeal to vacationing families. Wet 'N Wild, a water park next to the Sahara containing almost 2 million gallons of fresh water, was among the properties that precipitated the trend in 1984. Recreational vehicle parks, kids zones, motion rides, cinemas, and game arcades were introduced one after another. Circus-Circus added its Grand Slam Canyon Adventuredome in 1993—a magenta-roofed, air-conditioned, indoor amusement park. Not long after, the Sahara and New York-New York would feature roller-coasters to thrill guests. The World of Coca-Cola store appeared at the Showcase center on the Strip in 1997, fronted by a 100-foot-high Coke bottle and featuring a rock-climbing wall at its GameWorks inside. M&M's candies opened a shop right next door. In 1998, the Las Vegas Hilton launched Star Trek—The Experience, with its motion ride and museum of futuristic memorabilia. Mandalay Bay would open its Shark Reef, the Rio its *Titantic* exhibition, and the Venetian its Madame Tussauds "interactive" wax museum, one of only two in the United States. Indoor skydiving, go-cart tracks, trail rides, bungee-jumping, miniature golf, ice skating—a myriad of attractions were provided as recreational activities for visitors of all ages, convincing families to stay longer, spend more, and visit often.

Amidst all the entertainment, the appetites of visitors were not forgotten either: a plethora of restaurants began to pop up, many with themes. The Hard Rock Café was among the trend-setters. It was followed in quick succession by Planet Hollywood at Caesars Palace, the Harley Davidson Café just down the Strip, the Motown Café at New York-New York, and the Country Star Café with its huge jukebox in front. There was also Steven Spielberg's short-lived entrée into the restaurant business, the Dive, with its submarine replication. Opened later and still going strong are the Rainforest Café at the MGM Grand and the House of Blues at Mandalay Bay. West of the Strip, the city's own Chinatown developed, with numerous restaurants specializing in Far East cuisine.

Themes aside, truly gourmet establishments began springing up throughout Las Vegas, mainly concentrated in the hotel-casinos themselves, or close by. Previously, the two best known (and perhaps only) gourmet restaurants in town were Le Pamplemousse and Andre's, both specializing in French cuisine, located slightly off the tourist track in unimposing, redesigned older homes. Joining them in the 1990s were Spago's at Caesars Palace, Picasso at the Bellagio, Renoir at the Mirage, Drai's at the Barbary Coast, the Burgundy Room at Lady Luck, and The Top of the World at the Stratosphere—where guests can dine while gazing at a spectacular view of the city, as they slowly rotate 360 degrees in an hour's time. Along Flamingo Road to the east of the Strip, a row of stand-alone eateries also appeared, including Morton's steakhouse, Piero's trattoria, Bahama Breeze for tropical dining, Roy's for California cuisine, Hamada for Japanese specialties, Lawry's for prime rib, Cozymel's for coastal Mexican cuisine, and Buca di Beppo for family-style Italian food.

Culture and class were gradually making their way into the Las Vegas arena, too, as brought to national attention by the display of Steve Wynn's multimillion-dollar art collection at the Bellagio. By the turn of the new century, Las Vegas could boast of its own ballet troupe and philharmonic orchestra, the Nevada Opera Theatre, the Las Vegas Art Museum, and even a branch of the Guggenheim.

With focus shifting toward family recreation, shoppers were not forgotten either, as evidenced by the Boulevard, Meadows, and Galleria malls, the Belz Factory Outlet World at the far south end of Las Vegas Boulevard, and the Fashion Show Mall (completely renovated in 2002 at a cost of $362 million) right amid the Strip casinos. Competing with these were the stunning shopping arcades of the resorts themselves: Via Bellagio, The Forum Shops at Caesars, Desert Passage at the Aladdin, the Grand Canal Shoppes of the Venetian, Studio Walk at the MGM Grand, and the Tower Shops of the Stratosphere, being just a few of the properties added or expanded in the decade of the 1990s. From brand names to bargains, high fashion to low prices, the Las Vegas area now had it all—even the world's largest collection of new and used car lots, the sprawling Valley Automall in Henderson.

Another family attraction that continued to grow over the years was sports. Las Vegas developed major-league facilities, such as Sam Boyd Stadium, Cashman Field, and the Thomas and Mack Center. It began holding the Las Vegas Bowl for college football in 1992, spent $72 million to open the 1,100-acre Las Vegas Motor Speedway for drag, stock car, and formula car races (including NASCAR events) in 1996, and challenged the pros of the PGA Tour with its $5-million Invensys Golf Classic (formerly the Las Vegas Invitational). Andre Agassi became the city's best-known athlete in residence, a sports ambassador and local philanthropist. Boxing and rodeo still reigned supreme. Las Vegas would be home to a Triple-A baseball team (the Area 51s), have a one-season fling with the abandoned XFL (the Outlaws), indulge a brief affair with the fledgling International Basketball League (the No-Names), and convince the East Coast Hockey League to admit the Las Vegas Wranglers Professional Hockey team, owned by Charles Davenport, to play at the Orleans Arena from the fall of 2003. Nowhere, however, were the teams of the National Football League, the National Basketball Association, Major League Baseball, or the National Hockey League. The main reason Las Vegas never obtained a high-profile franchise, and most likely never will, was the proximity of gambling. Commissioners in the various professional sports organizations simply do not welcome any association with betting and especially not the Las Vegas sports books, whose money might somehow find its way into a local team or club.

Apart from tourists and new residents, Las Vegas also made moves in the 1990s to attract industry. Access to a reliable source of electric power (Hoover Dam), an educated and growing labor force, favorable tax laws (Nevada levies no corporate or individual income tax), and plenty of inexpensive space for expansion—those are the kinds of attributes corporations look for in evaluating locations for factories and offices, and Las Vegas had them all in spades. A massive business park sprang up south of McCarran Airport in the 1990s. Tenants include financial institutions and computer companies, as well as the administrative offices of many resorts.

As the culmination of a plan initiated during the late-1980s, in July 2000, Apex Industrial Park closed escrow on 10,000 acres of federal land northeast of Las Vegas off Interstate 15. The factory-zoned property soon attracted a number of manufacturing companies, including Republic Services, Georgia Pacific Corporation, Chemical Lime Company, Ulysses Corporation, and Kerr-McGee. Meanwhile, Jackson-Shaw Company was preparing to open the first phase of a $30-million 24-acre business park in North Las Vegas. Diversification of the region's tourism-dependent economy will be a point of key emphasis in the valley for decades to come.

The same can be said of water. Ever a concern in the desert environment, water became a problem of a new nature in the 1990s. Flows from Lake Mead were used to recharge the Las Vegas Valley's underground resources through tunneling known as a "straw." Refilling aquifers allowed the area's 9,000-odd wells to continue operating, but controlling the process was extremely difficult. Estimates of water needs depended very much on accurate projections of usage patterns. The population and number of visitors was growing so rapidly, requirements could not be accurately predicted. At times, there were shortages, requiring conservation measures until the straw could raise the underground water levels in the wells. In 1999, as demand fell short of the supply provided by pumping and natural replacement, an unexpected rise occurred in the water table, by as much as 30 to 40 feet in some places.

Mindful of the need to better regulate the supply, storage, and delivery of this precious resource, in the late 1990s the Water Authority launched into action a 30-year, $2-billion plan: the Southern Nevada Water System Improvements Project. It includes the construction of new pumping facilities, reservoirs, distribution pipes, water treatment facilities, and a second straw from Lake Mead. The latter was dedicated in 2000, a crucial step in ensuring adequate supplies of water in the valley in the years ahead.

Meanwhile, a studious effort was being made by casino owners in the 1990s to change the image of gambling itself. Betting activities were referred to as gaming and gamblers became known as players. Modeled after the frequent-flyer programs created by airlines, players' clubs became popular, with points awarded for play in lieu of mileage, redeemable for gifts, meals, rooms, shows, and even cash instead of free flights. Moreover, the games themselves evolved to attract more customers.

Until the 1980s, Las Vegas casinos' major income came from table games—craps, blackjack, roulette, and so on. Who would have guessed that a funny little invention by San Franciscan Charles Fey—the first slot machine, in 1895—would develop into the multibillion-dollar industry it is today? The "one-armed bandits," with their whirring cherries, oranges, and lemons, and "gigantic" payouts of $5, $10, or even $25, were once thought to appeal mainly to novices, the silver-haired ladies who sat glued to their machines for hours. People still sit glued to their machines, but now they face entrancing video screens with games alluding to popular television shows, movies, celebrities, and recreational activities . . . even fishing. This revolution in gambling was led by "video poker," a brainstorm invented by casino owner William "Si" Redd, which eventually evolved into the gaming giant, IGT. Cashless payout systems began replacing the clinking coin trays. Megabucks™ jackpots would invite slot players to become instant millionaires. The "green felt jungle" has given way to the electronic age.

Based on the renewed appeal of gaming and family entertainment, construction and renovation of casinos proliferated in the last decade of the twentieth century as the Strip made room for the Casino Royale; the Boardwalk Holiday Inn; the Monte Carlo; the Bellagio, with its lake, fountains, and Italian elegance; Mandalay Bay, with its tropical atmosphere, including a huge swimming area with man-made waves, and its adjoining Four Seasons Hotel; the Venetian, with its authentic recreation of Venice, Italy, including the famous canals, complete with gondolas and gondoliers; and the Paris Las Vegas Resort Casino, with an authentic, half-scale Eiffel Tower as its centerpiece. The latter five, with their "foreign" appeal, took Las Vegas Boulevard to new levels of elegance and sophistication, a far cry from the western-style gambling halls that originally put the Strip in business in the 1940s.

Beyond the Field of Dreams

Indicative of the trend to modernity, just off the Strip on Paradise Road, the world's first Hard Rock Hotel and Casino opened on March 10, 1995. Elsewhere in the valley, new gaming operations radiated in all directions—the Rio to the west of the Strip; the Fiesta, Texas Station, and Sunset Station in North Las Vegas; Boulder Station to the east; and Boomtown (later renamed the Silverado) to the south near Blue Diamond Highway. So imaginative, intriguing, and abundant were the new hotel-casinos of this decade, their older downtown competitors might not have survived had it not been for a bold plan to close a section of Casino Center to motor traffic and turn it into a unique venue—the Fremont Street Experience.

In 1992, architect Jon Jerde presented a plan to turn several blocks of Fremont Street into a covered pedestrian mall, dissimilar from urban renewal in other American cities in that the primary emphasis would be on entertainment, not shopping or commercial business. The sheer scale of the project also set it apart—$70 million in financing was required. The Las Vegas Convention and Visitors Authority pledged $8 million to the cause. New local room taxes and contributions from ten downtown casinos would have to cover the bulk of the cost. In 1993, the city received state approval to begin the proposed renovations, including a spectacular year-round light show under a five-block-long canopy, as well as beautification of the corridor to create a park-like public gathering center, with music piped in during the day and free evening concerts, street performances, and vendors selling their wares from small kiosks. These changes would bring to an end the 60-year-old Helldorado festivities in 1994 and replace them with a permanent attraction based on the future instead of the past. YESCO was once again heavily involved in creating the amazing attraction.

On September 7, 1994, vehicular traffic was permanently closed on the downtown street and, on September 8, an all-day party took place, celebrating the beginning of the Fremont Street Experience and honoring all the events that had taken place over the years on historical Fremont Street. Classic cars from the 1940s, 1950s, and 1960s cruised up and down the street, in tribute to what teenagers had done for many years as part of their "rites of passage" on this classic hometown street.

At record-breaking speed, the Fremont Street Experience was readied for opening and, on December 14, 1995, the official inauguration took place. Since then, the downtown area has again become a popular place for visitors, offering free seven-minute music and light shows every hour nightly on its innovative ceiling. On weekends, holidays, and for special occasions, there are often live bands playing as well as special exhibits. The Fremont Street Experience was listed among America's top ten places to be for Y2K celebrations, drawing a sell-out crowd to dance, drink, and cavort at the biggest Las Vegas block party ever held. It has breathed new life into Casino Center, drawing additional businesses—the Neonopolis commercial complex with restaurants, shops, and a multiplex cinema; the Neon Museum, preserving the vintage signage of eras gone by; and Jillian's entertainment-dining pavilion. It has spurred renewal nearby, too, including beautification projects for downtown Las Vegas, such as the Poet's Bridge on Lewis Avenue between Las Vegas Boulevard and Fourth Street. A sought-after venue for special events, the Fremont Street Experience will be the focal point of Las Vegas in May 2005, when the city fetes its centennial anniversary—especially fitting since this is exactly "where it all began," the site of the railroad station and the land auction held 100 years previous.

This transformation of Fremont Street saved the downtown and its casinos, but not every property in Las Vegas could survive the competition of the 1990s. The Landmark, which might be called "Hughes's Folly," was one of the properties Howard Hughes bought that never quite achieved the greatness it might have. Despite changes of ownership in later years, it still failed to break even. On November 7, 1995, the towering structure was carefully and dramatically imploded, but not without its last touch of glory. A few months previous it had been used for exterior shots, posing as the Tangiers Resort in the movie *Casino*. Its actual implosion was photographed and used by Tim Burton for his bizarre and entertaining film, *Mars Attacks*. In that movie, it was called the Galaxy. Many people mourned the hotel and remembered good times gambling, being entertained, and enjoying the spectacular view from its observation bar and restaurant. A year later, Las Vegas would lose another landmark as the Hacienda Hotel and Casino was imploded on December 31, 1996 to make way for Mandalay Bay.

Two properties suffered bankruptcy in the 1990s, but were spared the wrecking balls and dynamite. One was owned by Debbie Reynolds, a Hollywood icon very much identified with Las Vegas since the 1950s. She realized her dream of opening her own resort in 1993—the Debbie Reynolds Hollywood Hotel—which replaced the 1970s Paddlewheel just east of the Strip. Of key interest to the star was creating a place to display her extensive collection of Hollywood memorabilia, leading to the establishment of her own museum, adjacent to the hotel and casino. She put extensive funds, time, and effort into remodeling the older 180-room hotel. Despite her best efforts and that of her son Todd Fisher, the hotel finally filed for bankruptcy in 1997. A year later, the property was purchased by the World Wrestling Federation and renamed the Convention Center Drive Hotel in 1999. More recently, it has become the Greek Isles Hotel, under new ownership. The "unsinkable" Reynolds, meanwhile, continues to draw crowds, appearing on Las Vegas stages, including headline performances at the Orleans Hotel and Casino.

About this time, another troubled property was headed for take-over. The Stratosphere Tower, the tallest free-standing observation tower in the United States and the tallest structure west of the Mississippi River, had opened on April 30, 1996. Completed at a cost of $550 million, it was touted as the third most expensive hotel-casino project ever undertaken in Las Vegas. Huge crowds of tourists flocked to circle its 360-degree observation deck, but few stayed in its rooms or gambled in its casino. Owner Bob Stupak scrambled to promote the property, but the cash just would not flow fast enough.

In December 1996, Stupak defaulted on payments to bondholders who had put up the Stratosphere's construction funds. Subsequently, billionaire financier Carl Icahn bought up the bonds for pennies on the dollar and, upon approval of state authorities in mid-1998, assumed control of the monolithic hotel-casino. Soon after, he bought out Arizona Charlie's Hotel-Casino on the Westside and Sunrise Suites on Boulder Highway. Was Las Vegas about to witness a new Howard Hughes in action? Oddly enough, Icahn, like Hughes, had run Trans World Airlines. He was one of two casino owners (Kirk Kerkorian being the other) wealthy enough to purchase any gambling enterprise he wanted. By early 2002, the financier had studied more than 50 casino operations in southern Nevada. Unlike Hughes, however, Icahn has made his investments cautiously, putting off any further acquisitions and waiting for optimum circumstances. It remains to be seen what impact the presence of a new billionaire will have on the history of Las Vegas.

As the twentieth century was winding down, it seemed that Las Vegas might have reached its apogee as a gambling center. Casinos had popped up one after another on Native American reservations across the nation in the 1990s. States other than Nevada had moved to legalize gambling. Atlantic City had revitalized itself to attract the east coast's high-rollers. Even New Orleans had brought back riverboats to take players and their money up the old Mississippi. Many said that there was no need in Las Vegas for new hotel-casinos. Yet from 2000 through 2003, no fewer than eight major gaming properties opened their doors in the valley, including Terrible's on the site of the former Continental Hotel, the Palms just west of the Strip, the Suncoast in Summerlin, Green Valley Ranch Station in Henderson, the Hyatt's new casino and Casino MonteLago at Lake Las Vegas, the Cannery in North Las Vegas, and the new Aladdin right on the Strip. At Caesars Palace, a $65-million replica of the Roman Colosseum was topped off in mid-2002, readying for a new 2003 stage show starring Celine Dion. Late in 2002, ground was broken for yet another Strip resort, Le Reve, owned by Steve Wynn. It will be constructed on the site of the former Desert Inn and is scheduled to open in April 2005, just in time for the Las Vegas Centennial. Appropriately named in a place called "the meadows," Le Reve means "the dream."

Throughout its first century, Las Vegas has most certainly been a field of dreams. At times, it has seemed to defy gravity. Neither world wars nor economic depressions stunted the community's growth. Following the tragic events of September 11, 2001, however, many began to question the city's resilience.

On that terrible day, when New York's Twin Towers collapsed and the Pentagon burned, Las Vegas was paralyzed. The nation's airlines were grounded in the wake of terrorist attacks. Visitors were stranded here for up to three days before McCarran Airport was approved for resumption of flights. Tourism, not surprisingly, fell to a new low in the weeks that followed. Americans became afraid to travel. It would take months before hotel occupancy rates began to pick up again and, during that time, the area's resorts began laying off workers in huge numbers. The new $1.2-million Aladdin filed for bankruptcy. By October, nearly 6,000 jobs had been lost, unemployment in Clark County increased by one-third and reached 7.3 percent. Las Vegas ranked among the cities most badly affected for months after the attacks.

One Las Vegas resident, Barbara Edwards, a language teacher at Palo Verde High School, was a passenger aboard the airplane that hit the Pentagon. Even as local friends and students mourned her death, Las Vegans knew they had to do something. Local firefighters offered their assistance in digging through the rubble at the plane crash sites. Thousands of area residents went to blood banks and donated the only thing they could—the gift of life. Others contributed money and, together with local businesses, raised several million dollars in relief funds, much of which went to the Red Cross and charitable organizations on the east coast. A considerable portion, however, was used in Clark County to offset the devastating economic effects of diminished tourism and to support families cut off from incomes and healthcare benefits.

Tourists and jobs came back slowly to greater Las Vegas. Employment levels returned to normal only in the opening months of 2002, but in true Las Vegas fashion, the numbers have been climbing ever since. Optimism about the future is gradually growing with them.

To create an environment that provides quality living to 1.5 million people, the Las Vegas City and Clark County governments have initiated dozens of public works projects in the past few years. Parks have been added and improved, new senior centers opened, recreational facilities (such as swimming pools and community centers) renovated, and a library system created that could serve as a model for communities elsewhere in the nation.

The quality of public education is also being addressed. Under the leadership of Superintendent Carlos A. Garcia, the Clark County School District ranks among the country's six largest—with 262 schools, 12,625 licensed personnel, a quarter of a million students, a transportation network of 1,137 buses, and an annual operating budget of over $1 billion. Seventy-two new schools opened from 1996 to 2001 and dozens more are scheduled to go on stream by 2008. With the influx of non-English-speaking students into the system, emphasis on language learning has been made a key priority. In recent years, drop-out rates have been on the decline and Scholastic Aptitude Test scores have been holding steady. Many critics point to a lack of higher education opportunities in the Las Vegas area. As many as five new state colleges are needed here by 2010, according to a study by the Rand Corporation. Until then, the Community College of Southern Nevada and UNLV need to grow to meet increasing demand for post-secondary-school classes.

With 4,000 new residents moving to the valley each month and the number of visitors approaching 36 million annually, growing pains are inevitable. In the twenty-first century, Las Vegas faces the same urban concerns that other big American cities have experienced, notably rising crime, traffic congestion, and environmental issues. Gang violence has replaced the mob as the area's organized crime problem. Recent statistics have shown a decline in overall crime rates; in 1980, the figure was 10,743 crimes per 100,000 people and, by 1999, it had fallen to half that—just 4,591 crimes per 100,000. In 2002, the city was rated among the nation's ten safest cities with a population over half a million. But according to recent FBI figures, of the top five travel destinations in the United States, Las Vegas still ranks as the most dangerous. Improved and expanded law enforcement resources are needed to keep a 24-hour town safe for residents and visitors alike.

Negative headlines must be avoided, too, if the Mob image of the 1950s is ever to be buried. A local homicide case was recently sensationalized throughout the country, largely because it involved the kind of elements that sell tabloid newspapers and magazines: illicit drugs, infidelity, and hidden treasure. On September 17, 1998, Ted Binion, son of casino legend Benny Binion, was killed. After a long trial, those convicted of the murder were his girlfriend Sandy Murphy and her accomplice Rick Tabish. The story was made even more sensational because of the discovery of an untold fortune in mint silver dollars that Binion had collected since boyhood and kept in a desert vault in Pahrump. The existence of the loot became known publicly when Tabish was found digging it up soon after Binion's death.

Much like law enforcement and public relations efforts, local transportation networks must be expanded and improved. Tourism and population growth has drastically increased the number of motorists in the valley. The specter of gridlock is being addressed by plans for new roadways, including completion of the Beltway, which will circle Las Vegas to the west; rationalization of the Citizen's Area Transit (CAT) bus system; and the opening of a monorail to ease pedestrian and motor traffic along the Strip. When completed in 2004, the Las Vegas Monorail™ system will be the nation's first fully automated, urban monorail rapid transit system. Funded without public tax revenues, it will provide direct connecting service to eight major resort properties, as well as the Las Vegas Convention Center. The system will be open to the general public, providing a convenient and safe commuting alternative for local residents who work along the route. In its first year of operations, the monorail is expected to serve 19 million passengers.

Developments of this scale will give visionaries good reason to continue to bring their dreams to Las Vegas as the city's second century unfolds. Already on the table are plans for grand new Strip properties—a San Francisco-themed hotel-casino to replace the Frontier by 2006 and an out-of-this-world Moon resort designed by a Canadian consortium, if financial backing is available. To whisk visitors from California to the new attractions, a magnetically levitated, elevated monorail has been proposed. It would travel at speeds up to 240 miles per hour, cutting the land journey from Los Angeles via San Bernardino/Riverside to under two hours.

Futuristic, "other-worldly" projects seem to be a logical next step in the evolution of Las Vegas. Consider the city's already-existent association with Area 51, also known as

Groom Lake, a secret military facility about 90 miles north of Las Vegas. The number refers to a 6-by-10-mile tract of land, at the center of which is a large air base the federal government will not discuss. Since the mid-1950s, the site has been used for testing top-secret reconnaissance planes, owing to its remoteness, proximity to existing facilities, and the presence of a dry lake bed for landings. Groom Lake is America's traditional proving ground for "black budget" aircraft before they are publicly acknowledged. The facility and surrounding areas are also linked—with varying levels of credibility—to UFO and conspiracy stories. In 1989, Bob Lazar told a Las Vegas television station that he had worked with alien spacecraft at Papoose Lake, south of Area 51. Ever since, Area 51 has become a popular symbol for an alleged UFO cover-up by the federal government.

For many people, this science fiction imagery is already connected with Las Vegas, just like the atom bomb testing grounds, even though both areas are located at least 45 miles away. Local gift and souvenir shops routinely display "Little Alien" likenesses on magnets, postcards, and novelty items. No matter what is really going on in Area 51, it continues to fuel the imagination of many and add to the overall mystique of Las Vegas.

While looking to the future with hope, Las Vegans are also beginning to recognize the value of the past and the natural environment. In 1991, the Las Vegas City Council adopted the Historic Preservation Ordinance establishing the Historic Preservation Commission, an 11-member group of volunteers, deeming it responsible for developing, coordinating, and implementing programs for the preservation of buildings, structures, sites, and districts in the city that are of historic, cultural, and/or architectural significance. In 1997, the city council expanded the authority of the commission to review proposed landmarks or other structures located on a historic site or within a historic district. Such reviews are used to encourage property owners to pursue preservation alternatives and goals. Subsequently, numerous vintage properties have been added to the National Register of Historical Places, including the Las Vegas Hospital on Eighth Street, the Stephen R. Whitehead House on Seventh, and the Washington School in North Las Vegas.

Farther afield, the Clark County Parks and Community Service Division set about preserving the natural habitat by creating Wetlands Park, a 130-acre nature conservation site off Tropicana Boulevard east of Boulder Highway. Opened on April 21, 2001, the park provides a glimpse of the geographical and wildlife history of the region, while promising the restoration of a valuable natural resource. Trails, a stream, ponds, an amphitheater, and viewing blinds are just a few of the preserve's many features, giving visitors access to the unspoiled attractions of water, wildlife, and vegetation on the floor of the desert valley. This is where beavers once were plentiful, until heavy trapping in the mid-nineteenth century nearly caused them to die out. Now, the beaver population is slowly coming back and the balance of nature is being restored.

Meanwhile, the Las Vegas Valley Water District has undertaken a preservation project of an even grander nature, to restore Las Vegas Springs, which was designated as an archaeological site and listed on the National Register of Historical Places in 1978. The Las Vegas Springs Preserve (LVSP) is an ambitious public-private venture to create a showcase for the valley's history, complete with museums, gardens, walking paths, and restored structures that will tell the story of Las Vegas' past on the site where scout Rafael Rivera made his historic find. Scheduled to open in May 2005, LVSP will reconnect twenty-first-century Las Vegans with "the ancient people and early European explorers who found sustenance in the desert, despite its harsh realities."

If the Las Vegas Valley is to continue to bloom, it must not only preserve its natural past, but protect its environmental future as well. Perhaps the biggest threat to survival in the desert area is no longer flash floods, scorching heat, or lack of water, but human pollution, the intended creation of a "nuclear graveyard" at Yucca Mountain, 110 miles north of Las Vegas. The federal government had considered sites in Texas, Washington, and Minnesota as possible dumps for spent nuclear fuel, but in the 1990s, the choice was narrowed to southern Nevada. Tests have indicated that the location is safe for storage of radioactive material, but opponents have pointed out that the 10,000 or more tons of waste to be deposited at Yucca Mountain will not fully decay for 100 centuries—longer than the pyramids of Egypt have existed and then some. No assurances can be made convincing enough to win over local anti-nuclear activists. Litigation is expected to continue right up until the 2010 deadline for the start of waste transport to the site.

By that time, Clark County should have a population of just over 1.8 million. It currently ranks among the top 50 fastest growing counties in the United States and number one among all counties with a population of 1 million or more. The latest census (2000) shows Las Vegas, the city proper, has just under half a million residents, surrounded by nearly a dozen smaller communities. Bounding the city limits to the north is the incorporated city of North Las Vegas (population 115,488). To the east is the township of Sunrise Manor (156,120), to the west is Summerlin (3,735), and to the immediate south are the communities of Spring Valley (117,390), Paradise (186,070), and Winchester (26,958). Add to those the neighboring areas of Enterprise, Whitney, Green Valley, Nellis Air Force Base, Lone Mountain, Tule Springs, and the city of Henderson (175,381), and the greater Las Vegas metropolitan area currently claims roughly 1.4 million residents, making up the bulk of Clark County's citizenry.

According to the census data, twenty-first-century Las Vegas mirrors the make-up of the United States' population in an uncanny fashion. In terms of age, both the city and the nation count a quarter of their citizens under 18 and a little more than one-tenth 65 or older. In terms of sex, both split just about evenly. They also include comparable mixes of racial and ethnic groups.

Where once an African-American man could not even walk through a casino, an entrepreneur, Don Barden, now owns a major one—Fitzgerald's with 638 hotel rooms and a 42,000-square-foot gaming area. Where Mexican-Americans had all but disappeared from the scene 50 years earlier, Hispanics and Latinos are now by far the largest minority, accounting for approximately 22 percent of the Las Vegas population. Where Asians had previously been invisible, 1 in 20 residents is Asian-American (with Filipinos now the dominant group) and the Asian-American Political Action Committee plays a highly visible role in local election campaigns, their votes wooed by candidates from every political party. There is also a thriving gay, lesbian, bisexual, and transgender (GLBT) community in Las Vegas, with a 24-year-old biweekly news publication, the *Las Vegas Bugle*, and a GLBT center for support services and networking in operation since 1993.

The communities of people who built early Las Vegas continue to be major contributors to the local economy and social scene. The Latter-Day Saints now have an $18-million, 119-foot-tall temple at the base of Sunrise Mountain, and estimates put the Mormon population of Las Vegas at close to 100,000. Fourteen synagogues—from Orthodox to Messianic to Reform—are listed in the Las Vegas Valley, serving the area's diverse Jewish populace, who have active social groups for veterans, businesspeople, civic-minded women, and even singles. Since the 1960s, the Las Vegas Sons of Erin and the Las Vegas Daughters of Erin have celebrated Irish heritage locally. Daughters of the British Empire has brought together women with links to the British Isles and other Commonwealth countries. Greek Americans have gathered each autumn since the 1970s for an annual festival of food and culture, supported by the local Greek Orthodox Church. The Sons of Italy, the Grandsons of Italy in America, the Italian-American Club, the Italian Catholic Federation, the Augustus Society, and the Nevada Society of Italian-American Lawyers are just a few of many groups representing Italian Americans here.

Among these diverse groups, the one that has been in the area the longest, the Southern Paiute, is now among the smallest. The Las Vegas Colony numbered only 108 residents living in 37 housing units at the turn of the new century. Like their counterparts in other regions of the country, the local Paiute have used their special status as "a nation within a nation" to earn revenues, not from gambling, however, which in Las Vegas would give them no competitive advantage, but from the sale of tax-exempt cigarettes. Operating a smoke shop near Washington Avenue and Main Street, the tribe has been able to use profits to improve their reservation and create a Cultural Preservation Committee. They also used tribal funds to construct an 8-foot-high wall around the original 10 acres deeded by Helen Stewart back in 1911 to protect themselves from the surrounding city's rising crime rate. But that is not all the smoke shop income has allowed them to do.

Beyond the Field of Dreams

Back in December 1983, as part of a national reparations policy, a new law set aside 3,840 acres of federal land for the colony. The federal government took acreage north of the city into trust for the Las Vegas Paiute and, by the 1990s, proceeds from the smoke shop enabled them to create a small housing development there. In addition to a number of pleasant, one-story family homes, they also built a golf course that—designed by Pete Dye—has been ranked among the top ten in the nation by *Golf Digest*. Earnings from the 18-hole course in turn allowed them to develop a second course on the same range, and then open a third tournament-level course in November 2001. A business hotel (sans casino) and a fourth course are in the planning stages.

By hiring outside specialists and schooling themselves, the tribe gradually instituted its own police force and court of law, a social services agency, and an administrative office. Instead of elders or a chieftain, an elected seven-member council headed by a chairperson governs the Las Vegas Colony now. Tribal leaders still have serious concerns about the decline of their cultural traditions and native language, care of their elderly, and the education of their children, but they will readily admit that times are better now than they had been for decades. According to a nephew of former chairman Raymond Anderson, "We're right where we're supposed to be."

And so is Las Vegas as it comes to the conclusion of its fabulous first century and begins to embark on a new era of expansion and change. From dusty trail stop to railroad town, gateway to an engineering marvel and gambling capital, to the most entertaining city in the world, it has been a remarkable 100-year journey—one that seems destined to continue for as long as there is the water and the will to make desert dreams come true.

BIBLIOGRAPHY

Alley, John. *The Las Vegas Paiutes: A Short History*. Las Vegas: Las Vegas Tribe of Paiute Indians, 1977.

Balboni, Alan. *Beyond the Mafia: Italian Americans and the Development of Las Vegas*. Reno: University of Nevada Press, 1996.

Benson, Phillip L. *Southern Nevada Times: Southern Nevada History Before Legalized Gambling*. Las Vegas: Phillip L. Benson, Publisher, 1994.

Berman, Susan. *Easy Street*. New York: The Dial Press, 1981.

———. *Lady Las Vegas: The Inside Story Behind America's Neon Oasis*. New York: TV Books, Inc., 1996.

Best, Katharine and Katharine Hillyer. *Las Vegas—Playtown U.S.A.* New York: Van Rees Press, 1955.

Castleman, Deke. *Las Vegas* (Fourth Edition). Oakland: Compass American Guides, Fodor's Travel Publications, 1996.

Denton, Ralph. *A Liberal Conscience*. Reno: University of Nevada Oral History Program, 2001.

Denton, Sally and Roger Morris. *The Money and the Power: The Making of Las Vegas and Its Hold on America, 1947–2000*. New York: Alfred A. Knopf, 2001.

Dunar, Andrew J. and Dennis McBride. *Building Hoover Dam: An Oral History of the Great Depression*. New York: Twain Publishers, 1993.

Elgas, Thomas C. and Stanley W. Paher, ed. *Nevada: Official Bicentennial Book*. Las Vegas: Nevada Publications, 1976.

Elliott, Gary E. *The New Western Frontier: An Illustrated History of Greater Las Vegas*. Carlsbad, CA: Heritage Media Corp., 1999.

Elliott, Russell R. with William D. Rowley. *History of Nevada* (Second Edition, Revised). Lincoln: University of Nebraska Press, 1987.

———. *The WPA Guide to 1930s Nevada*. Reno: University of Nevada Press, 1991.

Finnerty, Margaret. *Del Webb: A Man. A Company*. Flagstaff: Heritage Publishers, 1991.

Glass, Mary Ellen. *Nevada's Turbulent 50s: Decade of Political and Economic Change*. Reno: University of Nevada Press, 1981.

Graham, Jefferson. *Vegas: Live and in Person*. New York: Abbeville Press, 1989.

Greenwood, Robert. *Nevada Post Card Album: Photographic Views of Nevada 1903–1928*. Reno: Fred Holabird Americana, 1998.

Hess, Alan. *Viva Las Vegas: After-Hours Architecture*. San Francisco: Chronicle Books, 1993.

Hopkins, A.D. and K.J. Evans. *The First 100 Portraits of the Men and Women Who Shaped Las Vegas*. Las Vegas: Huntington Press, 1999.

Bibliography

Howard, Anne Bail. *The Long Campaign: A Biography of Anne Martin*. Reno: University of Nevada Press, 1985.

Hulse, James W. *Lincoln County, Nevada: 1864–1909*. Reno: University of Nevada Press, 1971.

———. *The Nevada Adventure* (Sixth Edition). Reno: University of Nevada Press, 1990.

Jones, Florence Lee. *Water: A History of Las Vegas* (Volume II). Las Vegas: Las Vegas Valley Water District, 1975.

Knepp, Donn. *Las Vegas: The Entertainment Capital*. Menlo Park, CA: Sunset Books, 1987.

Land, Barbara and Myrick Land. *A Short History of Las Vegas*. Reno: University of Nevada Press, 1999.

Las Vegas Review-Journal. *Las Vegas—Through the Generations (A Pictorial Review)*. Marceline: D-Books Publishing, Inc., 1995.

Lewis, Georgia. *Las Vegas . . . The Way It Was*. Las Vegas: Las Vegas Sun Series, 1979.

Littlejohn, David. *The Real Las Vegas: Life Beyond the Strip*. New York: Oxford University Press, 1999.

Maggio, Frank. *Las Vegas Calling*. TAD Publishing, Ltd., 1975.

Martinez, Andres. *24/7—Living It Up and Doubling Down in the New Las Vegas*. New York: Villard Books, 1999.

McCracken, Robert D. *Las Vegas: The Great American Playground*. Fort Collins: Marion Street Publishing Company, 1996.

McMillan, James B. *Fighting Back: A Life in the Struggle for Civil Rights*. Reno: University of Nevada Oral History Program, 1997.

Miranda, M.L. *A History of Hispanics in Southern Nevada*. Reno: University of Nevada Press, 1997.

Moering, Eugene P. *Resort City in the Sunbelt—Las Vegas, 1930–1970*. Reno: University of Nevada Press, 1989.

Odessky, Dick. *Fly on the Wall: Recollections of Las Vegas' Good Old, Bad Old Days*. Las Vegas: Huntington Press, 1999.

Ostrander, Gilman M. *Nevada: The Great Rotten Borough 1859–1964*. New York: Alfred A. Knopf, 1966.

Overstreet, Everett Louis. *Black Steps in the Desert Sands*. Las Vegas: Native Son Bookstore, 1999.

Paher, Stanley W. *Las Vegas: As it Began—As it Grew*. Las Vegas: Nevada Publications, 1971.

Rathbun, Daniel C.B. *Nevada Military Place Names of the Indian Wars and Civil War*. Las Cruces, NM: Yucca Tree Press, 2002.

Reid, Ed. *Las Vegas: City Without Clocks*. Englewood Cliffs, NJ: Prentice-Hall, Inc., 1961.

Roske, Ralph J. *Las Vegas: A Desert Paradise*. Tulsa: Continental Heritage Press, 1986.

Rothman, Hal K. and Mike Davis, ed. *The Grit Beneath the Glitter: Tales from the Real Las Vegas*. Berkeley: University of California Press, 2001.

Rothman, Hal. *Neon Metropolis: How Las Vegas Started the Twenty-First Century*. New York: Routledge, 2002.

Shepperson, Wilbur S., ed. *East of Eden, West of Zion: Essays on Nevada*. Reno: University of Nevada Press, 1989.

———. *Restless Strangers: Nevada's Immigrants and Their Interpreters*. Reno: University of Nevada Press, 1970.

Sonnett, Robert. *Sonnett's Guide to Las Vegas*. Las Vegas: Robert Sonnett, 1969.

Stenn, David. *Clara Bow: Runnin' Wild*. New York: Cooper Square Press, 2000 (Revised). Original printing: 1988.

Stevens, *Joseph E. Hoover Dam: An American Adventure*. Norman: University of Oklahoma Press, 1988.

Swan & Laufer. *Neon Nevada*. Reno: University of Nevada Press, 1994.

Taylor, Lois A. *A History of the Clark County Heritage Museum: Yarns of Yesteryear*. Henderson, NV: Clark County Museum, 2000.

Taylor, Richard B. *Las Vegas Hacienda Hotel History—Supplement Edition*. Las Vegas: Beehive Press, 1990.

———. *Las Vegas Hacienda Hotel History Volume II*. Las Vegas: Beehive Press, 1998.

———. *Moulin Rouge—Hotel History*. Las Vegas: Beehive Press, 1995.

Thompson, David. *Nevada: A History of Changes*. Edited by Donald Dickerson. Reno: Grace Danberg Foundation, 1989.

Thompson, Thomas H. and Albert A. West. *History of Nevada 1881*. Berkeley: Howell-North, 1958.

Venturi, Robert, Denise Scott Brown, and Steven Izenour. *Learning from Las Vegas*. Cambridge: Massachusetts Institute of Technology, 1972, rev. 1994.

Ward, Kenric. *Saints in Babylon: Mormons and Las Vegas*. Las Vegas: 1st Books Library, 2002.

Weatherford, Mike. *Cult Vegas: The Weirdest! The Wildest! The Swingin'est Town on Earth!* Las Vegas: Huntington Press, 2001.

Wilkerson, W.R. III. *The Man Who Invented Las Vegas*. Beverly Hills: Ciro's Books, 2000.

Wilman, J. Catherene and James D. Reinhardt. *A Pictorial History of Nellis Air Force Base, 1941–1996*. Nellis AFB: Office of History HQ—Air Warfare Center, 1997.

Wright, Frank. *The Pioneering Adventure in Nevada*. Las Vegas: The Nevada Historical Society, 1987.

———. *World War II and the Emergence of Modern Las Vegas*. Las Vegas: The Nevada State Museum and Historical Society, 1991.

YESCO. *A Legacy of Light*. Salt Lake City: Young Electric Sign Company, Inc., 2001.

INDEX

159